they meant it
FOR EVIL

LUCINDA PENNINGTON

Tate Publishing & Enterprises

The opinions expressed by the author are not necessarily those of Tate Publishing, LLC.

Published by Tate Publishing & Enterprises, LLC
127 E. Trade Center Terrace | Mustang, Oklahoma 73064 USA
1.888.361.9473 | www.tatepublishing.com

Tate Publishing is committed to excellence in the publishing industry. The company reflects the philosophy established by the founders, based on Psalm 68:11,
"The Lord gave the word and great was the company of those who published it."

Published in the United States of America

ISBN: 978-1-61346-093-1
1. Religion: Christian Life, Women's Issues
2. Religion: Christian Life, Social Issues
11.07.11

they meant it
FOR EVIL

Overcome God's Way

Rom. 12:21

Lucinda Pennington

Dedication

I would like to dedicate this book to my heavenly Father, who promised me that "When my father and my mother forsake me, then the Lord will take me up" (Psalm 27:10), and He has throughout my life kept that promise. To my wonderful godly husband, Stephen Pennington, who stands with me without hesitation through all our good beautiful memories and also through our hard trials. He has always been my strength, encouraging me when I was not strong, helping me look to my Lord for healing.

To my four beautiful, loving daughters, Elisabeth Grace, Elizabeth Hope, Elysabeth Faith, and Elyzabeth Charity. My daughters continue to give me the strength and encouragement to carry on day after day, achieving the goals that I feel God has set for my life. Also to my adoptive mother: she was my encouragement and inspiration when everyone else in this world said that it could not be done. She would encourage me to always give my all in everything that I did. She taught me how to read and to write when the State of Maine said it was impossible. She taught me that there was nothing too hard to accomplish if you set your mind to it and put your trust and faith in God. She taught me to believe that you can do all things through Christ. I was encouraged by the strength my mother showed in the Lord. She fought a great battle with cancer; even up to the very end, she remained strong and true to her faith in God. Lord willing, my daughters will also see in me what I saw in my mother, and that is the will to obey and serve my heavenly Father in whatever comes my way, turn that which was meant for evil in my life and give it over to Christ and turn it into something good.

Table of Contents

Introduction

Warning: This book is very graphic and could trigger nightmares or fears for some of those who have been severely abused. Some triggers may be nightmares of their own past experiences surfacing due to reading some of my experiences. My advice is if you suffer from severe abuse and have not been able to deal with it, please find a friend to read this book with you and help you process your feelings.

This book is for those who want to see change in their lives, to overcome the pain of the abuse and heartaches in their lives. If you are reading this and know someone who needs help with anger and abuse issues, please give him or her a copy of this book. I believe this will help those who truly want to be helped. I do not tiptoe around any of the issues, so if you do not want to change or overcome from your abuse or heartaches in your life, this book is not for you.

The choice has always been yours: what will you do with your life? Will you allow yourself to be an angry, bitter, hateful person for the rest of your life, or will you be someone who will choose to overcome the past of abuse and make a life of what God wants for you, which is joy and happiness.

Please allow God to help you turn what was meant as evil in your life and allow Him to use you and turn what was meant for evil into something good for Him.

Show your abusers they did not ruin your life! Your abusers no longer have this power over you! Stand up and be proud you are a survivor! Praise Jesus!

This poem was written by my oldest daughter; she wanted to dedicate this poem to this book for you who have hurt inside like me for so many years.

She Bleeds Inside
By Elisabeth Grace Pennington (age 15)

She bleeds inside because she knows they're scared.
She bleeds inside because she cares.
Always keeping on a smile, if only for a little while.
Her thoughts are dark and wrong.
The tormenting devil that lingers is strong.
Bound by chains and barbed wire, she cries out,
"The man's a liar!"
She cries, but only at night, as not to give the young
ones fright.
Broken and abused.
Mistreated and misused.
She bleeds on the inside, because all of her emotions
she has to hide.

The Beginning

When I tell people about my past and they hear the horrible things that I have had to endure in my life growing up, they are shocked and horrified and find it difficult and very hard to believe because of the happiness and the stability that I have shown them in my own life today. They wonder how I could not be in a psychiatric ward or hate God and so-called Christians for the rest of my life for allowing such evil things to happen in my life, which were done by many who claimed the name of Christ. They want to know if I have ever turned to drugs or alcohol to cope with such pain from a past as mine. They wonder how I can get through with daily life after everything I have had to endure. How have I had seventeen years of a happy marriage and the ability to raise four beautiful daughters for the Lord?

All I can say to them is it is only by the grace of God and my strong faith and a one-on-one personal relationship with Christ that truly gets me through each and every day. I also share with them that I am a firm believer that God is in the recycling business and not the trash business. People are never truly ruined beyond repair. They may be broken for a little while, but they can be repaired and fixed. They are not to be thrown away or set aside as garbage because God can use all people who are willing to allow their lives to be touched and used by Him.

My goal in this short life given to me by the grace of God is to take what was meant for evil in my life to hurt and destroy me and cause me as much pain as possible and turn it around; I intend to use what was meant for evil in my life and turn it around to help others see Jesus through my painful yet joyful life.

I spent the first eleven years of my life listening to people telling me that I was worthless, mentally retarded, and that I would never amount to anything. I would not be able to do anything with my life because I was damaged goods and far beyond repair. Praise God, because with His help I have been able to do what I have dreamed of doing, and that is helping others heal from their painful wounds of past abuses. I continue every day to strive to meet a new goal or accomplishment, no matter how hard or how long it might be for me. It may take me a little longer to accomplish a goal in my life than it does for someone else, for example, finishing my education, but I keep on keeping the faith and my strength in my Lord and Savior. I will be done with two master's degrees someday, Lord willing, by 2012, but we will have to see it may take me a little longer.

I do have some learning disabilities, but I will not let that stop me from learning. It may take me a little longer than most people, but I am okay with that. It took me six years to learn how to write and receive a small business grant. My first grant proposal that I wrote, praise Jesus, was so well written that I received the grant money of twenty-five thousand dollars to start my own business in just three days.

I still have my home business even today. My daughters are co-owners/partners and help me. We sell books online; my business name is Homemakers Book Deals LLC. I am given the opportunity to share with others how to start their own business. It is exciting to hear when they are doing well.

I will have to admit that I do become discouraged at times in this weak flesh of mine. I remind myself that I am human, and we all hurt at times in our lives. Sometimes for reasons we don't even know because a sound, thoughts, smells have triggered bad memories for us. I have even struggled at times with feelings that I don't matter and that I am nothing in this small world. Sometimes I feel all alone and that no one cares that I even exist. I know as a mother sometimes I even feel unappreciated for all my hard work. But don't we all feel this way one time or another?

Many times throughout the years I have struggled with low self-esteem in this cruel world of what we like to call the workforce. Due to the lack of the my ability to confront conflict with my authority figures at work, I have even allowed my supervisors to abuse me verbally, emotionally, and even discriminate against me. At times I have felt weak and even all alone in this big corrupt world and felt unworthy of people's love and understanding. I still, to this day, struggle with making friends due to lack of having good friends as a child and being so isolated; I don't have the strong social skills needed to make lasting friendships. But I will also say I don't give up on this endeavor to learn how to make and have friends in the Lord.

When I am feeling down and out, that is when I quickly remind myself that God is not in the trash business but in the recycling business, and that no life is trash or unworthy; God has work for me to do here on this world of His.

I think the most important thing is that I remind myself that God never gives us more than we can handle or bear. God has trusted in me to do what is right, even when others around me are doing wrong. My purpose in this short life given to me is to tell and show others of this Jesus Christ I speak so highly of. I can't show what Christ has done for me in my life if I give up now!

God must think I am pretty strong to entrust me in the knowledge of how it feels to be used and abused. He trusted that I could handle it and overcome it and guide others to do the same through Him. There will always be evil people in this life hiding behind the name of Christ, but just because they claim the name "Christian," they will hear Christ say to them when they stand before Him at the judgment seat, "But he shall say, I tell you, I know you not whence ye are; depart from me, all [ye] workers of iniquity" (Luke 13:27). The one thing I take comfort in is God says that He will avenge the evil done to me. I know that God can do far worse than I could ever imagine to my abusers! The Bible even tells evil people you're better off with a millstone around your neck and thrown in the deepest sea than to hurt one of God's children.

This is a wonderful promise of God I have had to remind myself of often. In 2009, new sex offender registry laws in Maine allowed my adoptive father, the man who raped me, to no longer be on the national sex offender registry list.

When I found this out, I felt betrayed and hurt by the government. I had to remind myself that even when man's laws have failed the victims of sexual abuse like myself, God will punish this man and the many other wicked predators for the crimes they made against me and other innocent victims. Meanwhile, I have tried my best to petition the state of Maine to reconsider the victims in the process of changing their sex registry laws.

I am trying to get my voice heard; my goal is to protect other innocent victims from these horrible, wicked, evil predators who prey on children and adults. My abuser says I need to leave him alone and stop making the world know about him so he can get on with his life because I ruined his life! He says he could not get the job, the wife, and three daughters he almost had because they did not know about his other adopted daughter he molested and raped for many years. Shocker! I know; my adopted father almost remarried a woman that had three daughters.

I was working at Krispy Kreme Doughnuts in Greenville, South Carolina, at the time when I was called in from the back room where I was stuffing those delicious, cream-filled delights. A police officer needed to see me in the front of the store. This scared me just a little because I thought something bad had happened to my husband.

I came out to be greeted with a great big hug and an excited police officer saying, we were going to be family. I was a little confused because I knew my brother was already married. I figured it had to be someone from my new husband's side of the family. I told the police officer I had not met most of my husband's side of the family and did not know what he was talking about. He was still so excited; he said, "No, I am talking about your father." This also confused me because my birth father had been married for many years. I told him this, and he said, "Silly, I am talking about your adopted father; he is marring my sister tomorrow."

I told the police officer I was happy for his sister, but that man he was speaking of was not my father, and I told the police officer that I prayed that his sister never had children, especially any daughters. The police officer at this point got very upset and agitated with me because he told me she had three daughters and what a terrible thing to say.

I then very politely said, "You may want to do a background check on that man before your sister marries him, and you'll understand why I don't call him my father." The police officer tried to press me for more information. I informed the police officer I could not tell him anymore, but he could get all the information he needed from the national sex offender registry because my family would not be very happy with me if I told on him. The police officer left the Krispy Kreme doughnuts that day as he was walking out the building asking his police station to do a background check on that man.

The police officer came back the next morning crying and again with the hugging, thanking me for letting him know because everyone just assumed that my adopted father was a great godly man because his sister had met him at her church and never dreamed that he was a sex offender. The police officer told me his sister called off the wedding.

I reminded the police officer that I did not do anything, just told him to do a background check on him. He said he knew, but he would not have done that without me telling him about the national sex offender registry. You know what? My family was still so mad at me because I had done this. I had ruined my sex offender adopted father's life again!

I purposely did not tell the police officer my story or what my adopted father had done to me so my family would not blame me if she called the wedding off, but I had just referred him to the national sex offender registry. Sad to say, I cannot even do that anymore because he is not on the registry. Thanks to the new state laws about sex offenders being allowed to petition the courts after so many years of being on the registry and only having one victim or conviction, etc.

I did not even know that my adopted father was even getting married. I really did not care, but I believe God sent that police officer to talk with me that day because those precious daughters of that woman needed to be saved and protected from a predator. God does say, "Be sure your sins will find you out" (Numbers 32:23b).

I believe it was about a year later, in 1996, I was told that he did remarry a woman who did not have any children, and the reason I was not told of their marriage this time was so his new bride would not know about me and ruin his happy marriage, which, I was told, did not last very long when she found out about his past, which, by the way, she never found out by me; I'm not sure how she found out. I knew it would be a matter of time that she would find out.

What is so sad is that people marry sex offenders all the time and don't even suspect or know that their partner is a sex offender. Sex offenders are very good at looking the part of the nice, innocent, good, sometimes godly person; sex offenders are very good at deception. Now there are many states have allowed many sex offenders to come off the sex offender registry list.

There are many victims who do not even know that their offenders are no longer made to register because they do not inform the victims when they are allowed to petition to no longer register.

It is horrific because I know my abuser loves to seek out churches, and he still claims to be a born-again Christian! When I found out that I cannot refer people to the sex offender registry anymore, that was when I really had to talk to God and myself. I like to call this self-reassurance, a pep talk, if you want. We all know the saying, if you're given lemons in life, add some sweet sugar and make lemonade. That is when I decided this book, my life story, needed to be heard! I needed to find my voice, face my fear, and help other victims who are scared to come forward because the one who is abusing them are their godly fathers, brothers, uncles, etc.

I try to tell those I counsel that you must put your trust, your hopes, and even your dreams in Christ; there is nothing that you cannot do or accomplish in this life! I have them repeat this: "I can do all things through Christ!" (Philippians 4:13)

I even apply this to those who I have the privilege to counsel that do not claim to be a Christian; they can do anything if they believe that they are worthy of it. You have to believe and love yourself. I know sounds selfish, right, but if you do not love yourself, how you do expect others to love you?

When they are feeling the most down and out is when I tell them to look in the mirror and encourage themselves. I know it sounds silly, but I do this a lot. When I start getting discouraged and things start to get really hard and confusing for me, I take the time to look in the mirror and say to myself, "Lucinda, you have come way too far now to turn back. Keep up the good work. God will get you through this! Things have been worse in your life, and God has always got you through it; this thing you're facing is nothing! Now turn that frown into a smile and get moving forward for the Lord." I will talk to myself like this all the time.

I am always reminding myself that I make the day, the week, the year how I know God would want for me as a Christian. There are mornings that I wake up in a mean, ugly mood, not really sure why I am feeling so angry and frustrated, and the day has not even started yet. I started out on "the wrong side of the bed," as some like to call it.

I give myself a little pep talk in the mirror, and then I just might crawl back into the bed and ask God's forgiveness and get out on the other side of the bed and pep talk myself into having a better day. Remember, none of us is perfect, far from it. We all get angry, frustrated, hurt, lonely, scared at times in our daily lives, and these feelings come naturally to us; it is what you choose to do with these feelings that will make a difference in your life.

If you are having a bad day because you feel hurt or angry at someone, just forgive him or her, even if he or she does not ask for it, so you can have a better day. You may feel that person owes you an apology, or he or she may not even think he or she has done anything wrong to you. Life is too precious and way too short to fight the little stuff.

Believe me, sometimes it is easier said than done! Just remember this important key to contentment and happiness in your life: we are all sinners saved by the grace of God. We will not be perfect in this life. We are going to make huge mistakes. People are going to disappoint you and let you down. Yes, they are even going to hurt and make you distrust them. Just remember even you are going to make mistakes. God wants us to learn from our mistakes and get back up dust ourselves off and do what is right. Most important, remember you're not alone; others around you may feel the same.

The main thing I tell the teenagers and people I counsel is that the reason I am where I am today is because I chose to make my life what I want it to be (through the Lord's help, of course). If I get angry, I make the choice whether to forgive or stay angry.

And the second thing I tell my counselees is I will not allow my abusers to ruin or dictate my life for me. I will not give my abusers the satisfaction of hurting me any further. Now, none of my abusers have ever asked for my forgiveness; some even blame me for their lives being ruined because they received rebuke and consequences from the law for what they have done.

I will not sit and dwell on my past except to share when it will help someone else see that life is hard, but if I can be an overcomer, so can anyone who wants to! It has not been easy to overcome my past, and I will not lie to you or try to sugarcoat things; it has been and still is very hard, and I even now as an adult get through it only day by day with my faith and trust in my heavenly Father to help me. It is a daily process for me to keep my faith in my heavenly Father fresh.

It was not something I did overnight, and I will have to continue to overcome my past, my triggers, day by day, for the rest of my life. Life is hard, but with the encouragement from God's Word you can see through each and every day.

You will face trials, even failures! But you can overcome through the strength in God; you can overcome anything! I like to read these verses every day to encourage myself daily in the Lord! A pep talk to do right at all times no matter what comes my way!

> I can *do all things through Christ* which strengtheneth me.
>
> Philippians 4:13

> For it is written, As I live, saith the Lord, every knee shall bow to me, and every tongue shall confess to God. So then every one of us shall give account of himself to God.
>
> Romans 14:11-12

Be not overcome of evil, but overcome evil with good.

Romans 12:21

The Lord [is] my light and my salvation; whom shall I fear? the Lord [is] the strength of my life; of whom shall I be afraid?

Psalm 27:1

I encourage any woman who is striving to be a godly wife, mother, or employee to read Proverbs 31 every day. It will help you put your goals in prospective. I feel it helps me and encourages me in the Lord to do right.

My First and Second Foster Homes

My birth mother just up and walked out of the hospital, leaving me there at three days old. I was put into the state of Maine foster care until I was eleven years old. I don't remember much of anything about my first foster home except my fifth birthday because I was taken out of the first foster home on my fifth birthday. It also fell on Easter Sunday.

At the age of five, I was taken abruptly from my first foster home and put into my second foster home. In this home was when I experienced my first sexual traumatic nightmare that I can remember. I was being babysat by a teenage boy and his older sister during a wedding my foster parents left to go to.

My first sexual experience, I was told to close my eyes and

not to open them or he would cut my eyes out with the knife he carried in his pocket. I just remember when he was done doing his dirty deed I was hurting so bad and crying so hard. I remember a burning sensation, and I felt like something had cut me inside. I can remember it hurt to go to the bathroom; there was a lot of blood.

My older brother, who was placed in the same foster home at the time with me, came in and asked me why I was crying. I told my brother that the mean teen boy hurt me.

My brother asked me, "What did the babysitter do to you?" I told him I don't know exactly what he did, for I had to keep my eyes closed. He was on top of me, though, and he put something in me; I don't know what it was, but it hurt really bad, and I was bleeding, and I could not make the pain stop.

I told my brother the teen boy had his pants off when I opened my eyes for just a split second when I heard his belt buckle hit the bed because that sound meant I was about to get a whipping.

My foster parents at the time would use a belt that had a horrible belt buckle that hurt really bad when they beat me with it. When my foster parents came home that night, I was still crying on my bed. I told them and showed them the blood in my panties and told them of what the teenage boy did to me. To my horror, the foster mother did not even care; in fact, she laughed at me and said I was ready now and experienced and that her own son could do as he pleased with me. After that horrible day, I was made to have sex in her teenage son's room or in my own bed at night whenever he wanted me to.

I remember several times he had a sleepover with a few of his friends from his school, and they would take turns all night with me. Again I would wake up the next day in so much pain and soaked in my own blood.

This second foster home, I have to admit, was the most traumatic for me. I can't remember anything loving or good in this home—with the one exception: I was allowed to go to church on Sundays!

The abuse did not start out so terrible at first. The abuse really got worse after I was accused of killing my foster mother's autistic daughter, who had seizures all the time. I was only five or six years old when this event happened.

Her daughter was having a horrible seizure, and I tried to help the young girl hold her head up, for she was banging it so hard on the chair and the wall. I tried to wheel her away from the wall, but her wheelchair was locked, and I did not know how to unlock her wheels to move her.

So I continued to try to hold her head so she would stop banging it against the wall and her chair. My foster mother came in screaming at me, telling me not to touch her because if I held her head up she would swallow her tongue. Next thing I knew, the ambulance came and took her away. A couple of days later, they were all going to a funeral. I was forced to stay in the basement. I was blamed for my foster parents' teenage daughter's death, saying it was my fault. For many years

I believed I had deserved the punishments and abuse I received because I was an evil, wicked murderer! This was a heavy burden on my heart for many years!

The abuse became more cruel and sadistic after the death of their daughter. I remember my brother and I having to go hungry for many days. I remember eating dog food out of the dog dish, not enough for anyone to notice, because I did not want to get a beating or have to go longer without eating.

One time at school I stole the milk money out of my teacher's desk to buy food from a vending machine in the hall. I felt so guilty and so afraid that I would get caught, the thought of getting more days of no food scared me into giving my teacher the things I bought from the vending machine, and I asked for her forgiveness and begged her not to tell my foster mother! The teacher did not ask why I took it, but she let me eat one of the items for coming and telling her the truth about stealing the milk money out of her desk.

When my cruel foster mother felt that my brother and I had gone long enough without eating, she would put a pile of peanut butter sandwiches in front of my brother and I and give us about five minutes to eat as many as we could without anything to drink with them. You try to eat a pile of peanut butter sandwiches with no milk or water. The bread and peanut butter sticks to the top of your mouth, making it very hard to get much down.

Another time, my brother and I were so hungry we ate a watermelon out of the trash can, thinking nothing was wrong with it because it was a whole watermelon that had not been cut open, but we both got very sick from it because it was a very spoiled watermelon. I can't eat watermelon to this day without thinking about that time we got very sick off of it.

Another time I thought that I was evil or something like that because one year my foster family had gotten baby ducks for Easter, and I went out to pet them and play with them and love on them. I accidentally loved them to death. Literally, I hugged them and loved on them so much I had accidentally killed all of them. I did not understand that the reason they were not moving was because I had killed them.

I loved those fuzzy beautiful ducklings; I played with them all day until they stopped moving. I went crying to my foster mother that they were not moving.

I remember them telling my social worker when he came for his visit check-in that I was being punished because I was an evil, sick animal killer.

My punishment was to kneel on split fire wood with bare knees and hold out my arms straight out and hold about twenty plates without dropping them.

I remember my knees started to bleed from the cuts; I cried because the plates were getting too heavy, and I was scared that I would drop them and break them, and more punishment would be added.

My social worker just sat there sipping his coffee saying, "Well, you deserved it. Next time you will think twice before killing an animal." They loved to punish me for everything. They would get creative and more hurtful and sick with their punishments. Some of their punishments have left many emotional fears and many physical scars on my body and heart.

For example, I struggle to this day with an emotional fear of dirt basements. Actually, to put it more correctly, I have panic attacks; I am terrified of dirt basements. Just the smell of them will make me freak out. You will not ever see me crawl under a house or go in a dirt basement.

The reason for this fear: if I did something to annoy my foster mother or father, she would make me sleep in the dirt basement tied to the bottom of the star railing butt naked in the dark.

The reason she would tie me up butt naked was so that if I got loose from my ropes, I would not run away. I could feel things crawling on me and biting me. I would cry and plead for her to let me out. The more I cried to be let out, the longer she would leave me down in the basement, so I would just close my eyes hold my tongue and cry and pray to God to help me get through this. She would also put me down there when she went to the store or someplace that she did not want me coming along with her, especially the times my face or any part of my body that could be seen had black and blue marks on it from her hitting or beating on me. I hate and have a great emotional fear of dirt basements!

How does this affect me today as an adult?

My very first job I had, my boss wanted me to go into a dirt cellar to clean it out for her. She opened the door; the smell of that damp, musty cellar hit me like a ton of bricks, and I panicked and freaked out, crying and having a panic attack, refusing to go in the basement!

My boss called my chosen guardian, Mr. Andrews, who helped me get this job in the first place and told him I was fired because I would not go down that cellar and clean it. When Mr. Andrews came to get me, he pulled me aside and asked me to take a deep breath to calm down and tell him why I refused to do it.

I told Mr. Andrews how afraid I was of it and the reasons why. I was just in tears, begging my boss and Mr. Andrews to have me do something else, anything! I told them through my tears how sorry I was; I just could not go down there! When he explained to my boss why, she unfired me on the spot and said I could work in the garden instead. She even apologized for being so forceful with me and not understanding.

Another example of how their severe abuse affected my adult life: they damaged my heart due to physical abuse they did. How, you might ask. Well, the foster mother was well over three hundred and fifty pounds, and when I would do something wrong that she did not like, she would make me lie down on the floor, and she would put a kitchen chair on top of my chest and sit on it. I remember that I could hardly breathe when she would do this.

Due to this treatment, it caused so much pressure on my chest that it caused my heart to fuse to the wall of my chest. As an adult, I gained so much weight myself—363 pounds was my heaviest weight—that I went to see the doctor about why when I exercised I would faint.

The doctor checked and discovered that I could not exercise because the hole that I was born with in my heart would open up when I exercised from the pressure, and if I had not fainted, I would have bled to death.

When he discovered the damage done to my heart, he was horrified, even angered, that they could not do surgery to fix the hole in my heart due to my heart being fused to the wall of my chest due to my severe abuse. The doctor said if he even attempted the surgery, he would tear my heart in two.

I ended up having gastric bypass surgery to save my life, and I ended up losing over two hundred pounds, which took the pressure off my heart. Now my heart can heal the hole in my heart on its own. Praise Jesus, for He is so good to me. I struggle with my health, but the Lord is helping me heal and continue to grow in Him.

As a child, I had a problem of wetting the bed when I came into the second foster home. I don't know how long I had wet the bed, but I was five, and I would have accidents in the middle of the night. I was not allowed to get out of bed in the middle of the night or I would get beaten. I was also afraid of their son waking up and having a visit to my room. So if I woke up from having an accident, I would take my clothes out of my dresser and soak it up and put them back in the dresser.

If I happened to wake up just before I had my accident, I would wet the carpet next to my bed or wet in the closet in hopes to hide my accident. Remember, now, I was five years old at this time; I was terrified to get into trouble. I did not know what to do. I should have tried to sneak to the bathroom, I know, but I did not think of that at the time.

My foster mother could not understand why everything smelled like pee in my room and why the carpet was so wet and nasty. When she discovered what I had been doing, instead of spanking me or telling me it was okay to go to the bathroom at night, she decided she would teach me a lesson that I would not ever forget.

My punishment was for about a week. I had to sleep naked curled up in front of the toilet, and whenever she or anyone else in the house had to use the bathroom at night, they would pee on me instead of in the toilet. When I woke up in the morning, she would make me clean the floor up but not allow me to shower or bath. She would tell me to dress and go to school.

I got so horribly picked on and beat up over how smelly I was. Children can be the most cruel when it comes to making fun. I knew then that they just did not understand. I hid under my desk or wherever I could the whole week.

I never ever wet my bed as a child again after that horrible experience.

When I became a parent, one of my daughters had problems wetting the bed. I suggested to my husband to shame her in the wetting of the bed like I was. I told him what my foster parents did to me. My husband explained to me that was abuse and was not right, and this was not how we were going to teach our child not to wet the bed.

We helped her to wake up and use the bathroom. I was amazed that it worked; I was sure that the way it was done to me was the right way. That is when I went to my husband for any punishment or corrections with our children because I was afraid that I would do something wrong.

This foster family was sick and very perverted when it came to sex. It was not bad enough that I was made to have sex with her son and his friends. I had to endure my foster mother's many drunken parties.

The night before a party, she would put up naked pictures of men and women having sex and make me look at them; if I closed my eyes, she would burn me with her cigarettes all over my body.

Then during her parties the guests would have open sex with everyone. She would bring me in and strip me down naked, pushing me on her friends to have sex with them. I was made to have sex with men and women.

She would laugh and hand me what she claimed to be chocolate milk, but I would tell her it tasted bad. Come to find out years later, it was alcohol that looked like chocolate milk; I believe it is called brandy. Sometimes when she would have her parties I would hide outside in the bushes butt naked, hoping they would not miss me. I would see the police come to tell her to keep the noise down. I wanted to run to them for help but was scared what she would do to me if I ever told.

I did not know how to explain sometimes the bloody sores on my body when my teachers would ask me how I got them. I made up some really wild stories back then. Of course, I never told what really was happening to me because of the fear of what would happen if I did tell the truth. I knew if I did tell the truth, I would be punished even worse for telling.

My biggest coping skill at that time for me was just not to talk at all, be as silent and quiet as possible, and just maybe no one would notice me. My thoughts were just maybe if I did not bother my foster mother I would not get punished.

Sometimes I would hide at school after school was out, and I would get locked in the school. My foster mother did not care; she knew I was at the school, but when a teacher found me asleep in the school one morning, they made sure I was not hiding in the school after school was let out. The bus driver had to report every day to the school that I was dropped off at the door. He actually walked me to the door! I always wondered why my teachers and the many people who saw such bruises and a child who was so scared of her own shadow would not suspect abuse.

I am a Youth Specialist 2 for the Department of Social Services, and when I go to my trainings and I hear what the rules are and what we as mandate reporters are supposed to do, it angers me that no one did this for me as a child. It raises questions for me about the State of Maine's Department of Social Services praying they have improved since I was a child and the way they check out foster parents. I am glad they "train foster parents," but they don't really listen or check up on their foster kids. Well, at least in the first eleven years, I never felt like my social worker ever cared once for me.

Years later, when I read some of my paperwork from the DSS office, they wrote that they suspected abuse. Strangely, no one ever sat me down and talked to me about it or even asked me if I was being beaten or abused. I probably would not have told them at that age; in fact, I know I would not in fear of what would have happened after they left me there in the home.

You see, my social worker who came out to check on us would witness abuse, and he did nothing about it. I did not trust anyone! Another time, my social worker witnessed my foster mom putting me in the washing machine and turning it on and watching it spin me.

Instead of helping me, he would laugh and say, "Do it again!" I hated that man so much because he was supposed to be the one person I was supposed to be able to trust to care about my well-being, but I knew he did not care about me at all.

People have asked me why I did not just run away. Well, I actually tried to several times. I tried to run away to my birth father's home. He was about three miles away from my foster parents' house. I would get to the graveyard about a mile from his house and pass out with fright.

I could not get past that stupid graveyard for fear of it! My foster parents would find me and take me back to my abusive home. I wish now I had tried to run away in the daytime; maybe I could have gotten past that graveyard. Hey, I was kid; I never thought about it.

I know you're thinking, *Well, at least they were paid to give the foster children Christmas gifts and make that fun for them.* Sad to say, yes, they would buy lots of stuff, toys, clothes, etc.

They would not let me open but one toy and play with it, and the day after the social worker came out to see what they had given me, the foster mom packed it up, except for the opened toy, and took everything back to the store. If she was not angry with me, she would not break the toy she allowed me to play with. If we made her angry when our social worker came out, she would break the toy she allowed me to play with.

I would get visits from my birth mother once in a great while. One time when she was out she brought me a birthday cake and presents. When my foster mother got home that day and saw the cake and presents, she was angry because she was not asked if I could have the cake and presents. So she made me eat half the birthday cake and burned my gifts! I don't even know what the gifts were because she burned them in the wrapping paper. So birthdays were not even happy times for me. I don't ever remember a party or anything.

A Moment of Happiness in the Midst of Abuse

I know that all these stories I have told you in the previous chapter are horrific and terrible and hard to swallow. I assure you those are just a few experiences I believe will not traumatize you; there are many more I could share. Some things are just too painful and horrible to share. At this time I don't think it would be appropriate to share in this book. I think you get the point, though, of that second foster home and how they treated me.

What I want to share with you is the one thing that brought me great joy and happiness in this second foster home: the fact they let me go to church on a big, yellow church bus.

I absolutely loved it. I got to spend the whole Sunday at

church with people who treated me like they loved me. They were always kind and compassionate with me. They never made fun of my smell or my dirty, unkempt hair. They did not make fun or hit or punish me. They never called me names or put their hands on me. Most important for me is that they did not hurt me in any way. I knew that I was safe at church, for there was no fear of pain. I felt safe enough that I would sing and talk with only those I trusted.

The bus captain was so faithful to pick me up, rain or shine. I would wait so long to see that big, yellow bus come around the corner with such excitement. He would always have something for me to eat. So those times that I went without eating, I knew that if I was hungry on Sunday, my bus captain would have a treat for me. I don't think my bus captain ever knew that I had not eaten for several days.

I know I smelled horrible because I don't remember having to bathe much. At school I was teased and beat up on a regular basis for being smelly all the time. That was the main reason I acted out at school. I had learned very quickly if I screamed, hollered, yelled, or bit people, they would just leave me alone.

One time my bus captain actually got in trouble because that week my foster mother was not going to let me go church that week as a punishment for something I had done earlier in the week. But I snuck outside just before the bus was to come and ran to the bus when it arrived and told my bus captain, "Let's go."

My foster mother was sleeping and did not want to be bothered.

Well, when he brought me home that day, he got an earful from my foster mother about how dare he pick me up without her permission, etc. She even threatened my bus captain to call the police on him.

When my bus captain left that day, I got a bloody beating for sneaking out of the house. She beat me with anything she could put her hands on. She even burned my Bible and the vest with all the buttons and ribbons I had earned from the church's Awana program. It broke my heart, and my body was broken, but deep down it was well worth the beating and the pain. I felt loved that day at church! I would even today take that beating again.

I loved church, still do today. I am a Baptist pastor's wife today. I loved the feeling that those people at the church cared about me with not expecting anything from me in return.

They fed me, gave me Kool-Aid, and told me about this Jesus who loved me so much that there was nothing I could do to make Him not love me. They told me verses about how when your mother and father forsake you, this Jesus promises to love you more! "When my father and my mother forsake me, then the LORD will take me up" (Psalm 27:5).

I loved my bus captain and his family. I wish today I knew where he was and what his name was. I remember his oldest son's name because I loved him so much.

I had a crazy little girl crush on him. I wanted to grow up and marry him one day.

He was a teenager at the time, working side by side with his father. He called me "My beautiful blue-eyed and green-eyed princess." You see, my left eye is half green and half blue. He made me feel so special without hurting me. This bus captain and his family showed me what true love for Christ was.

What is the most special to me is that every foster home I went to, my bus captain somehow would find me just by knocking on every door he could for Jesus. I am so thankful for a faithful servant of Christ who made it his goal to knock on every door and tell others about Jesus and bring as many children as he possibly could to salvation and love of Jesus.

I don't know where this wonderful Christian family is today. I know that when I get to heaven, Jesus will tell them, "Well done, my good and *faithful* servant."

When I had the opportunity to go to Hyles Anderson College under a work scholarship offered to me by Mrs. Evens, a professor from the college who came to a Bible conference being held at the church I was currently attending, I made sure that I signed up to work in the bus ministry so I could learn what was so important about children for Jesus. I wanted to understand firsthand how to love others for Jesus. I received such a joy and a blessing on every Saturday, knocking on doors inviting children to come to church.

I enjoyed the many hours on Sunday helping other children see Jesus. I did not care how bad a child smelled or if he or she was dirty. They reminded myself of me when I was a bus kid. I knew many of my children lived in homes where they did not have much food to eat. I knew several of my bus kids had not eaten for several days.

So my friends and I would spend our Saturday nights making peanut butter and jelly sandwiches for my bus kids, who I knew would be very hungry on Sunday. I was on a work scholarship, so the cash I received was for tithes; I would use my tithes to buy the supplies to feed my bus kids. When I was asked where my tithes were and why they were not seeing them in the church offering, I told them what I was doing with it. I was informed that was not the proper way to tithe, that I had to put my tithe money in the offering plate on Sunday, not spend it where I thought it should go.

So I obeyed and was heartbroken about not being able to feed my bus children anymore. Praise the Lord; those who saw me spending my Saturday nights making lunches for the bus children started a money jar for my bus children so I could continue feeding my bus children on Sundays.

One thing I have learned throughout these many years is that when God closes a door and you're obedient to your authority when they are not asking you to sin against God, then He always opens another door.

My Third
Foster Home

This home was supposed not to have ever happened. I was taken in the middle of the night in my sleep. The Department of Social Services office did not even know where I was for several months. I was almost seven at this time, I believe. My foster mother, who had me from three days old from the hospital, took me from the second foster home because she said she could not stand how I was being treated.

When she saw the bruises and how unhappy I was, she wrapped me up in a blanket, told me to hush, and she laid me in the backseat of her car and told me to keep my head down. I woke up the next day in her home. This woman, I believe, truly loved me and thought I was her baby because she picked me up at the hospital when I was three days old. Remember, she had me until my fifth birthday.

Sad to say, she did not know, though, that her daughter was an evil teenage girl who was abusive to me when I was in her care. She would baby sit many children in the neighborhood when her mom was at work. She liked to play sick, perverted games with the children she would watch.

She would get us children split up in twos. Then she would tell us to watch the porn movie she put in and copy what we saw in the movie with whoever she paired us up with. She would punish those who did not do what we were supposed to do. She would burn our genitals with her cigarette. The rewards were sticks of sugar and other sweets.

It was horrible and a form of torture! I still wonder to this day if any of the other kids said anything to their parents or ever told on that wicked girl! I really pray that they never remember it!

When she wanted to go out with her boyfriend but she was told to watch me, she would put a diaper on me and take the racks out of the oven and put me in the oven and lock it. I was so scared that when they came in they would forget I was in there and turn the oven on. This gives me nightmares still about being burned alive!

Again, this affected me in my adult life. About seven months after I had gotten married, they had on the news a story about a man putting a young child in the oven and how he burned her to death out of hate for the girl's mother. It was the same apartment building that I was in as a child when I was put in the oven. When I saw it on the news, I could not stop crying. My husband could not understand why I was so distraught when he came home from work that day. I did not know how to tell my poor husband what was wrong.

That night I even wet my bed; I scared my husband; I was about six months pregnant with my first child, and he thought my water broke. I hated to have to admit to him that I had wet the bed. This was the first time since I was a small child that I wet the bed. My husband did not know what was wrong with me. After a few days of wetting the bed, we sat down and talked about it. He was so horrified to hear such fear from me. He was horrified and angry to hear what someone could do to me. He wept with me and comforted me, showed me the love and compassion I needed. He encouraged me with the love of Jesus. We prayed for that little girl who died in that oven. He helped me through that traumatic memory by reminding me that God protected me and that nothing could hurt me now. I have had several memories that were very traumatic for me to work through over many years. It is wonderful to have a godly husband who is a great support in my corner.

Sometimes I just need to talk about things; my husband will listen then tell me how much he loves me and how he will do everything in his power to never let me get hurt ever again. I have nothing to fear anymore!

I praise Jesus, for God blessed me with a good, godly, understanding husband.

It is important in your life to find someone positive to be there just to hear you cry and tell him or her over and over what bothers and makes you hurt. So when you are done spilling your guts out, he or she can uplift you, make you feel safe, and wipe away your tears. Having someone to remind you that Jesus loves you and cares for you is very important.

In this third/first home I was finally found by my birth father. He and the social worker showed up to get me from this third foster home. I was so happy; I thought my dad was taking me home for good to live with him. But instead I was sent to a group home until my father could have me. He only had me a couple of weeks. The state of Maine would not let me stay with my birth father. I was then sent back to the second foster home where my brother was still at. My brother and I were separated a lot. I suspect he suffered as well, but I can't say what they did to him because I don't know.

I never understood why they sent me back to the second foster home, for I wanted to be with my birth father. I felt that he protected me when no one else would. The weeks that I was with my dad, one of my other older brothers living in his home was caught hurting me sexually after my dad left to go to work. My dad had forgotten something and came back to the house when he walked in on my brother hurting me; he grabbed him off me and threw him out his front door and told him to never come back.

I remember my father saying he was blessed that is all he did; he should be sent to jail. I don't know how old my brother was; I think he was about fifteen, but I never saw him again until years later as an adult. My dad had hoped that I had forgotten this, but sad to say, some things you just can't ever forget. Like I said, I was taken from my father's and taken back to the second foster home. This made the sixth move for me.

I would go to the public school with horrible cuts and bruises. I would hide all the time under desks or behind the couch, away from the other children. I was in the special education classes because I was labeled mentally retarded due to my behavior at school. I can understand today why they labeled me mentally retarded because I acted crazy toward students and to the teachers when I wanted to be left alone. I did not want to be with the other children, so I would make a production of kicking, screaming, biting, and not talking to anyone I did not trust. So they put me in the special class away from the other students. I did not have to do any schoolwork, just look at picture books and sleep most of the day.

At recess I would hide in the concrete tubes so the other children would not beat me up for smelling so horrible. The children would ask me all the time where the bruises and cuts were from. Of course, I never told really what was happening at home. I was too scared that they would tell on me for telling on my foster parents.

Destroying Innocence
By Elisabeth "Grace" Pennington (age 15)
Dedicated to my mother, who overcame such great
odds in life.

My playmates were pain and tears.
Dreams were filled with hate and fears.
Toys? I had none.
I never had an ounce of fun.
Children should be held and loved,
Never pushed and never shoved.
My innocence they took from me.
That's not the way it should be.
It shouldn't hurt to be a child.

My Fourth
Foster Home

I slipped up one day when I arrived at school late due to one of my beatings in the third placement home. I saw my brother in his classroom due to his classroom door being wide open; he was looking at me wondering if I was okay. I whispered too loud, I guess, that I was okay. I told my brother, "I only got a beating; no blood this time." The teacher heard me and took me to the office immediately and called the police. They checked my back, and the next thing I knew, my brother and I were leaving the school, going to another foster home.

I did not know whether to be happy or scared to death. I had not had very good experiences with foster homes. I was happy that it was not a group home though. I did not like group homes; they scared me because of the other children were mean and hateful to me. Well, I was so excited when I arrived at this home; there were other foster kids my age. I figured she must be a good parent if they trusted her with so many kids.

This home was sort of good in their own way. The foster mother loved to paint and make ceramics, so we had fun painting and learning art abilities that we did not know we even had.

They did have their many faults. For example, when it was Christmas time, the foster kids had to wait until their family opened their Christmas presents first; then the foster kids could come in and open their gifts. I liked the fact that we actually got to keep the presents given to us in this home.

When they had any family function, everyone knew we were the foster kids and we were not to be treated as family. I loved the fact that I had my own bed, my own stuff; I did not have to share or worry about them taking it away from me. I still acted out at school sometimes because I was so afraid of the bullies.

But Christmas presents and not feeling a part of the family was the least of the problems. The main problem in this home was the older foster teenage boy would sexually abuse us younger girls. We were all too afraid to tell because he would threaten to hurt us if we told. He got caught one time with the other foster girl, and he got sent away immediately. I was so glad of this because I did not like him at all. I don't know what ever happened to him. I do pray for him, though, that he is not a sex offender still today.

One time they had family come and visit. My foster dad's father and his wife came to visit. The old man took me behind the shed and forcefully raped me with a hand tool from the shed. This man terrified me and hurt me severely. He came into my room that night to hurt me again, but he stepped on a toy and ran out of the room, afraid he would get caught by someone in the house. What I think is weird is he died a few days later. Everyone was shocked of his sudden death. Come to find out, he used to be in his younger years a preacher. I believe from this day God took him home for what he did to me. I don't know; maybe it was just his time. But deep down I felt like God had taken care of me.

The sad thing is this foster home couple ended up getting a divorce due to the father molesting us young girls in the home. So the foster kids and the others were split up. This family let me stay with the mother while they tried to find us another home to go to.

This foster mother let me go to church when the bus captain who picked me up since I was five found me again. He drove by one day when I was outside playing; of course he stopped and asked my foster mother if I could go to church. I wish I could find him and his family and let them know how much that meant to me.

I knew whatever home that the Department of Social Services put me in, he would find me and take me to church. This foster mother also allowed me to be in the dance classes at the public school. I loved to dance. I felt like a princess in my dancing outfits.

Now that I am grown, I have a hard time hearing that someone is a foster parent. The main reason for this feeling is I never had a good foster home experience to speak highly of.

One time I was sitting in a revival meeting with my husband, and I heard the preacher introduce his family. "This is my wife, my children, and my foster son." I got very upset. Of course, my husband did not understand why I would be so upset about how he introduced his family.

So I explained to him that he is letting everyone know that he is not his son, just in case he embarrasses him or acts out; it is not his fault because he is just a foster kid. So after the service I went to that preacher after he preached and shared with him how I grew up in foster homes.

I told him how he could get better behavior from his foster child if he would love him and make him feel like he belonged to the family. The reason I did this was because he mentioned in his sermon that sometimes when he gets foster children they misbehave, and he sometimes does not understand them.

I told him when he introduces them the way he does, he lets them know they don't belong. They are living up to his expectations, and that is for them to fail. I told him to try loving them as his own children and see how they respond to feeling like they belong and loved. A few weeks later, I received a thank-you letter from the preacher telling me what a big behavioral change he saw in his son. He no longer introduced him as a foster child but as his son. The preacher said he was pleased to say that the first Sunday he did not introduce his son as "foster child" was the day their son asked him and his wife if he could call them mom and dad. I had felt so blessed and overjoyed to hear I had helped this family.

More Than You Know
By Grace Pennington

I have been told I cannot learn.
To them mentally retarded was the concern.
They pushed, pulled, and pried
Till I broke down and began to cry.
Labels are wrong to place on a little child.
Children can act out, sometimes become a little wild.
Someday they will be able to show you
Children know more than you will ever know.

Adopted at Age Eleven

I was adopted at age eleven by my Sunday school teacher and her husband, who was a deacon of the church, who also had been a principal of the Christian school. The very first night in my adoption home he raped me. He told me that this is what I was supposed to do if I was going to be a good daughter. I had been raped since I was five years old. I did not know having sex with your father was wrong. I was never taught about sex and proper touching.

I was taught about dos and don'ts in a Christians walk and how children are to obey their parents without question in this home! My adopted mother believed that idle hands were the devil's workshop, so she made sure I learned all I could. I learned how to crochet, sew, cook, garden, clean, and work very hard on our small farm. I was taught how to play the piano and the flute, which I am very grateful about the piano lessons now because I can use this talent in my husband's church he pastors.

The church we attended taught Christian conformity. If you don't act, dress, speak a certain way, then you are not a true Christian. I did everything expected of me; I obeyed my parents, respected them, obeyed their rules; I did everything they asked of me.

My adopted father kept me from having too many friends; he said they were bad influences on me, and those I was allowed to play with were heavily monitored; I was never left alone with anyone. He was afraid, I guess, I would talk to them about what he did to me almost every night. I played volleyball in school, but my mother attended all my games. I sat with her on the bus; never alone with anyone was my adopted father's rule.

Due to my choice not to do much talking to others and my severe bad behaviors in the public schools, the State of Maine Department of Social Services had placed a label on me saying that I was mentally retarded and that I could not learn.

So my adopted mother, who had been a teacher for about nineteen years, sat me down and showed me what my picture in the adoption book said. I was just horrified when she read it to me! It went something like this:

"Lucinda Tibbitts is a quiet, shy girl who has been abused and emotionally scarred beyond repair; she is mentally retarded and cannot learn. She is in need of a special family who can help her and love her."

My adopted mother challenged me to change this stupid label that Department of Social Services placed on me. She told me it would take a lot of hard work, but if I was willing, she would do everything she could to teach me. I started learning from my mother how to read and write.

I could not believe what my mother was saying at first because I really put her through the ringer the first three days in her home. My first three days in my new adopted home, I acted like an infant baby. I insisted that I drink from a bottle. I insisted on wearing a diaper and making my new adopted mother change me— the whole works. I know the reason now as an adult why I did this. My reasoning at the time was so that my adopted mother could experience having a baby. I can see now as an adult I was testing her to see if she really wanted me and would do anything to show me that she loved me, no matter how terrible and horrible I behaved. The third day I was pretending to sleep in her lap, and she was praying softly that God would show this little girl how much she loved her and that there was nothing this girl could do to change that love. After listening to her prayer and realizing how much she truly loved me, I decided then that I was done pretending to be a baby.

My adopted mother did not care how I behaved or what it would take; she knew she loved and wanted me and wanted to help me be successful, so my first year I had been homeschooled from the time I got up in the morning until I went to bed at night.

Praise Jesus, the next year I went to the regular Christian school. I was still getting sexually raped every night by my spiritual, Christian, adopted father.

I was going to a Christian school, where sex never came up! It was never told to me that it was wrong or what it was. My mother never sat down and discussed sex with me and about it being wrong for people to not touch me in certain places.

At the age of fourteen, my adopted mother, who gave piano lessons, got a call one day; my best friend from school's mom needed my mother to watch her for one night due to a family emergency!

So I had my first sleepover. My best friend was in the bed next to me; I told her to hide under the covers when my dad came in because he has said no to anyone sleeping over. My dad came in touched and kissed me, then did what he did every night. My friend made her presence known when he started touching me inappropriately. He quickly left my room when he realized I was not alone.

When he left my room, my friend came out of the covers, crying, asking me if this was what he did every night. I said, "Of course. Doesn't your daddy?" She was so horrified and actually got angry at me for saying such a thing. We then had a long talk about sex; she showed me the definition of *sex* in the dictionary, and the next day at school she gave me a book about it.

She told me that if I did not tell my mom, she was going to the school principal and to the pastor. I begged her not to do this. I did not want to lose my family and be sent away. I did not want to break what I thought was good. I finally told my friend that I told my mother and she confronted my father and they both promised that it would never happen again. Of course, I lied to her so she would not tell on me.

What really happened was I was so scared I actually ran away to my last foster home mom's house and asked her what to do. My dad was doing bad things to me. He, of course, showed up at the door. He knew that would be the only place I would go because I knew no one else.

I would not tell the foster mother what he did to me; I just wanted to know what to do to stop it. Because I could not tell her, she let my adopted dad in, and he took me home. We stopped at the bottom of the hill, and he pulled over and wanted to know why I was trying to destroy our family.

I explained to him what I had learned and that what he was doing to me was wrong, and I was scared that I could have a baby by him because my friend showed me what he was doing was what caused a woman to get pregnant. I also told him I found out that daddies don't have sex with their daughters. I told him he had to stop it.

He told me I could not get pregnant because the vitamins he gave me every night were pills to keep me from getting pregnant, and he always used protection.

But he promised that he would not do it again. He did stop molesting me for a little while.

A few weeks later, he started molesting me again, telling me that I would lose my mother because she would believe him over me any day. If I told anyone, my mother would not love or want me anymore.

My mother's best friend's daughter was my friend; she spent the night several times but did not sleep in the bed with me. My mother set her up in the living room with the couch that opened into a bed.

One morning I came down to see her crying; I asked her what was wrong, and she said that my father had touched her the night before. He did not have sex with her, but he had touched her. I was so upset! I cried with her and told her what he did with me.

I told her that I would not let it happen to her again. I confronted him about it.

Of course, he just got angry at me and told me if I wanted to protect her from him, then I had to stop complaining and fighting him and give him whatever he wanted, which, of course, I did without question.

Another friend of mine was talking with me one day at school when she saw me crying on the school grounds, and I mentioned that I almost lost my family due to my other friend who said she would tell a secret of mine. And that in a way I wished that she had told someone because I could never tell now because I had to protect my best friend, but if I told maybe the wrong things the secret would stop. This friend was older than me, and she convinced me to share with her my secret. She was horrified and said that this could not be kept silent and that the proper people needed to be told.

I told her she would not be my friend if she told. She confronted me again in the hallway later that day and told me I had until the last study hall to tell the pastor.

I told her I understood what she was saying, but I begged her not to ruin my life; she cried and hugged me and told me I would thank her one day, and, as promised, the last study hall she went to the school principal and to the pastor. I was called in the office. I had to face for the first time in my life the realization I was being abused, and I had to tell my mother that I loved so much!

My principal confronted me; I could not lie; I cried my eyes out, but he took me that day to my adopted mother, who, of course, would not believe it! That was a horrible day—so much yelling and chaos. Way too much *conflict*! It terrified me.

I told her that I could not keep it a secret anymore because he had touched my best friend, and I was afraid that he would hurt my best friend. My best friend, who slept on the couch, was confronted, and she told her mother what she had told me.

I was begged by my adopted father to say my friend and I were lying and we were just making it up! He told me that he would stop and never do it again. So I said to the police officer and my adopted mother that I had lied, and that my best friend was making it all up. My friend almost never spoke to me again!

My friend is in heaven now due to a horrible car accident, but if I could speak to her today, I would hug her and thank her for having the courage to tell me and her mother what this sex offender had done to her and that I am sorry for not telling on him sooner; maybe she would have been spared the abuse.

That summer I was sent away to a family friend of my adopted parents, who spent the whole time telling me how evil I was and how I was going to burn in hell for saying such horrible things about my godly parents! I did not mind all the verbal abuse; at least I was not getting beaten and sexually assaulted every night. I was actually okay and content with the verbal abuse.

The Delight of Destruction
By Grace Pennington

Hit, beaten, mocked.
I was almost shocked.
My day began like any other,
But ended when I received a brand new mother.
I was overjoyed! No pain!
No more!
But all came to a halt when
The man she had married walked through the door.
For this demon of a man would hurt me in every
way
And that Is how my jubilations became that of
dismay.

Hephzibah House: Girls' Home for Troubled Teens

After the summer was over, my adopted mother told me about Hephzibah House, a girls' home in Warsaw, Indiana, and asked me if I would go there for a short time until things could cool down and people could forget about all about my horrible lies about my adopted father! My mother told me that Hephzibah House was a boarding school and that I would make lots of new friends like the books she read to me every night before bed.

Of course I wanted to go; it sounded exciting! I helped her pack my belongings, excited about a new beginning for me, and when I arrived at Hephzibah House I was relieved to be out of that abusive home. The day I arrived, I helped the staff unpack my bags and was so obedient to all they requested of me; I did exactly as I was told with no questions of why. I was taught from my adopted home to do what my authority asked of me, which was to obey right away! I was quick to learn it was not like any boarding school in the books my mother ever read to me. Hephzibah House is a place where they take troubled girls and under loving guidance in a structured environment do what they can to help them go on to live a life were they can grow and mature into a fulfilling and productive life for themselves and Christ. They had a lot of rules and structure to keep all the girls who came through their home safe from themselves and others.

A few days after arriving at Hephzibah House, the director of the girls' home, Ron Williams, called me up in his office and he sat me down and asked me why I was at Hephzibah House.

Hephzibah House was a home for rebellious, troubled girls who needed to learn about Jesus and obedience. I started with the rehearsed lines my mother gave me to say when I was asked. These were the reasons why I was there! I went on to tell of the many made-up reasons I was told to give to anyone that would ask me. Ron Williams said that yes, that is what my parents wrote down for all the reasons that I was there. He then asked me again; this time he wanted me to speak the truth! He told me that I was not displaying any signs of being a rebellious teenage girl.

I had just decided the night before from my bunk, after hearing a dramatized audio tape about hell, that

I would never, ever tell anyone again unless he or she specifically asked me about the abuse my adopted father had done to me; because I accepted Jesus Christ into my heart that night, I would not lie, but I would never tell anyone again.

Ron Williams leaned forward in his chair and told me that I could tell him anything. He said he would trust and believe in me; I had nothing to be afraid of. I broke down and told him the real reason I was sent to Hephzibah House and that my adopted father had sexually abused me. I explained to him how my adopted father had touched my best friend and about my other friend telling at my school, and that was the real reason why I was sent to Hephzibah House. He then told me I could prove that what I was saying was true if I wanted to! I told him I would like to do that because I was afraid that my adopted father would hurt someone else.

The director of Hephzibah House had his eldest daughter take me to the police station the next morning to take a lie detector test, which, of course, I passed. Immediately my adopted father was arrested because Ron Williams called the authorities in the state of Maine! My adopted father was arrested, but he was allowed to live at home under house arrest because I was safe at Hephzibah House.

Even though I loved and cherished Hephzibah House, I still feel that I served my adopted father's time, locked away from the outside world. Instead of my adopted father being locked up, he was allowed to live in his home and report to his parole officer. I felt that he was able to have all the comforts of home for a crime he committed, yet I had to be locked up for my own safety from him.

The hardest rule for me was about having communication back home at Hephzibah House. During their stay, the girls were not allowed to have communication with their friends. They were allowed just their mother and father (in my case, it was just my mother), siblings, and your pastor from back home.

God knew that where I was. I was reminded of my younger belief as a small child that when my parents forsake me, God will take me up! Ron Williams would talk with me when he came home from preaching engagements and counseled with me about some of my intense abuse growing up. He would help me work through my abuse step by step, accepting that bad things happen to good people, that God allows only what He knows I could handle, not easy to swallow at the time!

But you know, my walk with Christ grew on its own because of the loving counsel I received at the girls' home! I listened to the preaching and the teachings taught at Hephzibah House. Instead of dwelling on the negative of being away from family and friends, I chose to learn what I could of the Lord for myself. This is what I have done; yes, I have used some of what he taught in my adult life. I found words of wisdom very helpful throughout the years.

I have to admit that sometimes it was difficult for me at Hephzibah House; don't get me wrong; I wanted to have a family to go home to just like the other girls had. I had only two visits from my adopted mother in the three years I spent at Hephzibah House. I struggled with feelings of jealousy, anger, and resentment toward the other girls in the home. But I also experienced much joy, happiness, and excitement, for we had themed birthday parties every month for that month's birthday girls. I enjoyed the yearly carnival that took months to plan. I loved Hephzibah House; it felt wonderful and safe to me.

I was one of the needy girls because my parents were not able to send me things that I needed each month. I knew my parents could not afford the monthly payments for my room and board and spend money to come and visit me. Even though my parents could not pay, I was not sent away, which I was so thankful for. The staff let me crochet to pay for things I needed and wanted. I would make all kinds of different things. I loved it because it made me feel like I had something I could give back to them for all they had done for me.

Once when I was crocheting, Ron Williams eldest daughter, who had seen my work, asked if I would help with her wedding. I had the privilege to make his eldest daughter's wedding decorations. She loved the decorations I made, and she bought me all kinds of things for doing this for her. I loved the new shoes, the beautiful hair ribbons, and the new clothes.

She made me feel so good about my talent; I felt so responsible and appreciated for the work I had done. I still even today love to crochet and make beautiful things.

Most important to me during my stay at Hephzibah House was that they helped me grow spiritually with my walk with my Lord. I learned how to have a deep personal relationship with my heavenly Father. I chose to glean what I could from a situation that was beyond my control. I was taught that we make our own path; no one can define us! This is what I learned from Hephzibah House: *no one* but *God* tells us what to do! We submit, or we don't. We answer for how we behave and what we do in this life! We can't blame our past or the abuse to not serve the Jesus who gave so much for us. He gave His life for me.

The least I can do is live right and praise *Him*. Ron Williams helped me work through many of my childhood abuses that I shared with him. The abuse that I had to endure, I was able to understand, was wrong and was not my fault!

The director of Hephzibah House taught me that I could wallow in my own self-pity about the abuse I had to endure in my past, or I could put it behind me and put Christ first in my life.

Ron Williams taught me, through God's Word, that I can't change the past. I can use my past for Jesus by helping others. I could go through life blaming the many families for all my mess-ups, but I knew God already knew and expected me to forgive and put the past behind me. Jesus had done so much more for me then to wallow in my own self-pity!

I learned that I did not have to ask God, "Why me? Why was I so abused?" I shared few incidents that happened in my life with Director Ron Williams, but the truth and wisdom he shared with me through God's Word helped me trust in Jesus. You can be an overcomer, but you first have to make that choice to do this by forgiving your abusers. It is not easy to wipe away the tears and say, "Okay, that is the past; I was unloved, unwanted, abused, hurt, but Jesus is bigger than any of that."

This group home, Hephzibah House, for me, was a safe haven. It was a place for me to learn for myself that God loves me no matter what I have to endure on this earth! I felt so completely safe at Hephzibah House I could flourish in the Lord, for I never felt hungry, I felt completely safe from harm, and I never had to be afraid while I was there.

Hephzibah House staff taught me that nothing I could do can change *His* love for me. They taught me that it was okay to be angry and sin not.

This is where I learned that screaming at someone does not help a situation. I struggled with watching other students first come in yelling and screaming and being disrespectful to the staff ladies, and I learned the concept and witnessed that a soft answer turns away wrath.

I struggled with some things, but it was nothing that God could not help me through! I can do all things through Christ! I know it has taken me many years to look back at my stay at Hephzibah House, and I in all honesty can't say with all the abuse I have experienced in my life growing up did I ever feel so secure and safe in my whole childhood than what I felt when I lived at Hephzibah House.

Hephzibah House gave me so many tools that I have been able to use in my life today. They taught me anything I wanted to learn. I learned how to cook for a large amount of people, sew quilts, gardening, and so much more. Due to the things I learned at Hephzibah House, I have had the great rare opportunity to have many unique jobs over the years that I would never have gotten if it had not been for the things I learned at Hephzibah House.

For example, I was the first female maintenance worker when I went to Hyles Anderson College on a work scholarship. With all the skills I had learned, I could do a lot of work that a maintenance worker normally would have to get a female to tag along with him while he worked in the girls' dorms. But because I could do certain skills, I could do it and save them time.

I praise Jesus so much for the opportunity He gave me those three years in this girls' home to blossom and grow in the Lord. Ron Williams and his wife, throughout the years, have kept in contact with me and prayed for me all these many years! They taught me to love the Lord for myself! Even today I call them just to have them pray for me and thank them for being faithful to Jesus.

Here I Am

By Grace Pennington

Here I am,
Locked away.
Here I am,
Forced to stay.
Here I am,
With a group of strangers.
Here I am,
Trying not to cry.
Here I am,
Begging why?
Here I am,
A momentary rest.
Here I am,
Strangely blessed.
Here I am,
Afraid to leave.
Here I am,
With my heart on my sleeve.
Here I am,
Tired of pain.
Here I am,
Trying to stay sane.
Here I am,
Wishing the demons would leave me alone.
Here I am,

Still not my own.
Here I am,
Safe for now.
Here I am,
Wondering how?
Here I am and here I wish I could stay.
But the demons took me away.

My Life after Hephzibah House

The day I left Hephzibah House was so fast; I was not asked if I wanted to go home to my family or what I wanted to do with my life. My adoptive mother insisted on taking me home. I know the director of the girls' home did not want me to go with her. He tried talking to her and made several other suggestions, like letting me stay, even though they did not keep girls who were over eighteen that were not staff. I could stay until I finished high school or allow me to go live with my grandmother in Florida, but my mother insisted and demanded that I leave with her immediately. Deep down, I really was scared to death to go back home. I was afraid that my adopted father would abuse me again and afraid that I would not have the strength to fight him. My mother assured me that he had changed and that he would not touch me again. My mother promised she would protect me. So I was obedient as I had been taught to do and went back home without a fuss.

Not even a week after being back home, my adopted father started talking about the counseling sessions he had to go to during the time I was at Hephzibah House. And how they had told him sometimes he had to do what he did that was wrong and confront it afterward. I did not understand what on earth he was talking about. That night he came into my room and used starter fluid on a mask, which paralyzed me, and he raped me.

After waking up the next morning, I went down to breakfast; I tried to tell my mother what he had done to me the night before because she told me on the drive home from Hephzibah House that if it ever happened again, all I had to do is tell her and she would protect me.

Well, I came downstairs for breakfast, told my mother through my tears I needed to talk with her, and before I could say anything she slammed her hand down on the counter and said, "Lucinda, if it ever happens again between you and your father, it will be your fault, and I will never forgive you."

I was horrified, scared of what to say next. I did not want my mother to blame me. I had done nothing wrong. It was against my will, and yet if it happened again, she would never forgive me. I did not know what to do or what to say. My father pulled me aside that morning and told me that if I tried to tell her again, he would hurt her. And if she were to die, he would make me marry him because I was not his daughter. Later in the week, when I came home from school, I found my mother crying, saying that she almost got killed that morning; her brakes would not work, and she had almost crashed. When she had the car towed to the mechanic, she was told that someone had cut her brakes. The look I saw from my adopted father assured me that we both knew who had cut her brakes. I was now bound by the fear that he would hurt my mother if I did not allow him to do as he pleased with me. I would cry, quote scriptures, and beg him not to touch me.

He would tie me up, gag me, and hurt me where it could not be seen by others. Then when he finished his dirty deed, he would make me pray with him for forgiveness of his/our sin. I would go to school so many days just crying and weeping from the shame I had to endure before arriving at school.

My school principal, Mr. Andrews, several times pulled me aside, asking me what was wrong; all I could say was nothing. He never gave up, though, trying to find out what was wrong with me. He noticed that I was never allowed to have friends, and if I went to a teen activity, my parents were there as well. Whenever I was allowed to do anything, my parents were always there.

The school that year planned for a senior trip into the mountains where we went skiing. Even at nineteen my father was not going to let me go but was talked into it, saying it was my senior year and I deserved to participate. He warned me to keep my mouth shut! Enjoy the trip and stay to myself. This is what I tried to do. I was going up the ski lift when my school principle asked if he could hitch a ride. Of course I said, "Sure, why not." On the trip up the slope, he started asking me questions about Hephzibah House and why I was sent there. I tried to answer him as little as I could so as not to get into trouble with my parents. I told him I was sent away because I was rebellious and that the home was for rebellious teenage girls.

He told me he did not believe that I was rebellious; he knew me before I left for Hephzibah House, and I was the most obedient child he had ever meet. He continued to ask questions, which I tried hard to not answer. I told him that I could not tell him the real reasons why I was sent away and that he could not and would not understand.

He was not happy with my answer because apparently he did some research and found out the real reason why I was sent to Hephzibah House. And he found out that my adopted father had molested me for several years before going to Hephzibah House.

So about a week after the ski trip, he called my adopted father and asked if I could for about an hour come to his house and help with several other teens get something done at his house before bad weather came. I am not really sure how they convinced my dad to let me go. I was surprised he even allowed it. Mrs.

Andrews would pick me up and drop me back off. My principal promised my adopted father it would not take long and he really needed my help. So my adopted father allowed his wife to pick me up.

Mrs. Andrews stopped at a gas station and turned the car off and turned to me and, without hesitation, asked me if my father was molesting me again. I was shocked by her direct question but of course responded, "*No, of course not.*" I could not look at her eyes when I answered this because I was afraid she would see that I was lying.

I turned my head away from her and started to cry. She said she and her husband found out the real reason why I was sent away to Hephzibah House, and it was not because I was rebellious but because my adopted father had molested me.

She said she believed the many times I came to school crying were the days my adopted father had dropped me off at the school. And if my adopted father was molesting me, she and her husband could protect me and help me. I burst into tears, looked at her with anger because of what she said, and asked her, "How could you help me? Hephzibah could not protect and help me from that man, and my father would never allow me to leave the home. My mother would never forgive me. I have no place to go no one to help me. I don't have a job; I don't have a place to live, nowhere to go."

So I asked her what could she and her husband do to help me; my adopted father expected me home within the hour, and he would come looking for me and take me back home. She said that she and her husband suspected as much and had made arrangements to hide me from him until the proper authorities could be contacted.

I was scared to death, but she had convinced me that she and her husband would help and protect me. So I told her the truth; I broke down and begged her to help me; I did not want to be abused any more, but I did not want my mother to be hurt by him either.

I told her that my mother would not understand and would hate me. She assured me that was not going to happen. This family was an angel of hope for me. They took me in their home as one of their own. They got me my first job. They taught me how to drive. They sacrificed so much to help me, and I will be eternally grateful to them. My adopted father was arrested, put in jail for little less than three months. This family stayed by my side in all the court proceedings. They were my strength that I needed to get through the toughest time in my life. God knew I needed them. I believe that God sent them to me after praying for so long for the guidance to get out of this nightmare of abuse. My adopted mother did not forgive me and would have nothing to do with me for over two years.

This was a very difficult time for me, so I trusted completely in this family for their help and guidance. They took me to the pastor of their church at the time to discuss what had happened, and this pastor's reasoning was I needed to be church disciplined for being nineteen and old enough to know better and having sex with my father, because my father was a man of God! I had to have done something to make him fall into sin. I obeyed and went before the church as requested, even before my peers that I went to school with, and explained that I had been having sex with my father. Only one elderly lady stood up crying, saying how this was so wrong that I was a victim and what they were making me do was so wrong. The pastor told her to have a seat, that he knew what he was doing. This is one of those churches that the flock follows without questions. I am so thankful this family that took me in is no longer with this church. They did not like what was done to me, but we followed the rules the church put down for me. No helping in Sunday school or singing specials. I was no longer allowed to hang out with the teens until my allotted time was up, no longer bringing bus kids to church.

People ask me why don't I hate church and just give up on God. I had so many Christians who abused me, and people just treat me so wrong. Why don't I hate God? God was so horrible to allow Christian people to do such terrible, hurtful things to me. I have to say that, yes, God allowed these things to happen. When I stand before God one day, I don't want to waste my life and time on this earth allowing the evil done to me to dictate how I live for Christ when God has sacrificed the ultimate for me.

I can't blame my abusive past for not serving the Lord! It breaks my heart when I hear people say, "I used to love God, but there was a hypocrite in our church who turned me away from God." God has been so gracious and paid the ultimate sacrifice for us; it is sad to allow someone's mistakes take the joy of the Lord away from your life. I think maybe some people are just looking for an excuse to not serve the Lord. I see it as the least I can do is help others who have suffered, as I have seen that there is great light at the end.

That is why I love my job so much. I know it is not in a Christian home that I work for but a juvenile facility for teenage boys who are in trouble with the law. Many who come through the facility are teens who have suffered severe abuse and need compassion and understanding and someone they can learn to trust again.

I do get to work with many, and we see their wild behaviors, which they act out just like I did as a child when I wanted to be left alone. I understand them because I used to do the same behaviors growing up. They don't know about my past, but they do tell me that they sense that I truly understand them and I help them understand themselves.

I love God not because of so-called claimed Christians; I have a personal, one-on-one relationship and walk with Him daily; my trust in Him is not based on so-called Christians. These so-called Christians who sinned against me will answer for what they did to me when they stand before my Jesus one day.

Right now, here on this earth, I want to bring honor and glory to God and walk in His light, not a label of Christian, but someone who truly loves Jesus. I know it is easy for people to hide behind religion to sin. I don't believe everyone who claims to be a Christian even loves God or knows God. It is easy to play the blame game in our lives.

Your abuser does not care what they have done to you and how it will impact the rest of your life. They are selfish and evil; they are simply wicked, and they do not deserve your sorrow or pain. You are better than they will ever be. And they will be punished for what they have done to you. You may not see their punishment here on this earth in your lifetime. But watch when they stand before Christ and have to answer for what they did to you!

No one will be wiping their tears away! God says they are better off having a millstone around their necks and dumped into the deepest sea if they even think about hurting His child. And remember that is what you are; you're His! Show those around you He make you strong.

> It were better for him that a millstone were hanged about his neck, and he cast into the sea, than that he should offend one of these little ones. Take heed to yourselves: if thy brother trespass against thee, rebuke him, and if he repent, forgive him. And if he trespass against thee seven times in a day, and seven times in a day turn again to thee, saying, I repent; thou shalt forgive him.
>
> Luke 17:2-4

And, of course, I was right; my mother would have nothing to do with me at this point. She would return all my letters; all correspondences she would send back to sender. My adopted mother did exactly what I feared the most, and that was to hate and abandon me. All my life all I wanted was that mother-daughter bond. But in order to get the help I needed, I had to give that up.

I asked this family if they would mind helping me change my last name because I no longer wanted my adopted father's last name or his name on my birth certificate. They agreed to help me with this. I did not know what last name to use, so I asked if they would mind if I used theirs. They said they would be honored if I took their last name.

So at the age of nineteen, I changed my last name and appealed the courts to remove my adopted father from my birth certificate as my father. The courts granted my request, and my name became Lucinda Grace Andrews. This family not only took me into their home, but they treated me as an adult, teaching me responsibility of holding a job, saving my money for college. They helped me get a bank account in my name, teaching me how to be responsible for money. They spent time teaching me how to drive a car. They expected nothing from me in return, only to do my very best and trust in the Lord.

The day I went to my first driving test, I failed the test, and we had just left the Department of Motor Vehicles. I was driving very upset, of course, because I had failed the test. We were going through a green light, and I did not see the logging truck in time to stop; he had run a red light and side-hit us. This terrified me, and I did everything I could to keep control of the vehicle. I could have killed this man's children. I destroyed his family vehicle.

I was sure he would hate me and kick me out of his house. But instead he showed me love and compassion and understanding and said we were all fine and the vehicle was just a material thing; he was grateful to God and thankful that no one was hurt.

That night on the way to church, he threw me the keys to his big bee truck and told me to drive the family to church. I cried and cried, begging him to never let me drive again. I almost killed his family earlier that day; how could he trust me to drive again?

He assured me that it was an accident; it was not my fault the truck had run the red light, and he told me not to be afraid. I could not do it. He told me his family would sit there until I drove them to church, that if I did not drive again, my fear would overcome me and I would never have the courage to drive again. Through much tears I drove that huge truck to the church, scared to death, my feet barely able to reach the clutch, but when we arrived safely, I realized he was right; if I had not have driven, I would have never been able to drive again. I could never repay this family the car that got wrecked or their many sacrifices they made to keep me up in their home.

The Andrews family taught me how to trust again, how to see my strength was in the Lord, and there was nothing I could not do. I trusted this family so much. Even though I only spent a few months in their home, it seemed so much longer for me, for I felt like I had grown up so many years in just a few months.

I would encourage others to step out of their comfort zone if they know or suspect a person is getting abused. Ask yourself if there is anything you can do to help that person. This family did not have to help me; they had no obligation to do anything for me. The Andrews sacrificed so much to help me: time, money, their home; they were hated by many for helping me. They encouraged me to go to college and get a degree. That is exactly what I did. I now have a bachelor's degree in biblical counseling. I am still working on finishing my MS in biblical counseling and a MA in family counseling.

They helped me as if I were one of their own children. I praise the Lord for them daily. I believe they were the answer to many of my prayers. They did not judge me and blame me for my abuse. They just decided that they were going to help me no matter what the cost. I could never repay them for what they have done for me. But I firmly believe God will bless them richly for what they did for me. If not here on this earth, I believe they will be richly rewarded in heaven one day.

What God Expects
from Me Now

So many people have asked me how I do it. How do I
put the past behind me and move forward in my life?
My favorite Bible verse is, "Forgetting those things
which are behind and reaching forth unto those things
which are before" (Philippians 3:13b). How can I go
through life and not hate the church or God for allowing such horrible things to happen to me? This is what
my response to that question: What does the Bible tell
me to do? What does God want from me? This is what
I believe to be true. I am to strive to be a godly woman.
The following are some tips I would like to
share with you to use on how to become
this kind of godly woman that the
Bible teaches us about.

Step 1: Seek praise from our heavenly Father, not from men or our peers. Romans 2:29 talks of someone who is not just following a bunch of rules and regulations but who has a true change of heart: "Whoever has that kind of change seeks praise (commendation) from God, not from people." Seeking God to say, "Well done my good and faithful servant" (Matthew 25:21) will result in a truly fulfilled, attractive woman who is not needy because all of her needs have been met through Christ.

Women are emotional creatures; we seek praise and comfort from others; we need to look to Christ for our praise and comfort.

Step 2: Don't have the victim mentality. Yes, you need to cry your eyes out; then wipe away your many tears. What is done is done, and that is the past now; we have to move forward. The best part about the godly woman described in Proverbs 31 is that she is a competent woman. I believe she would be the same godly woman whether she was married or single. She never blames her circumstances or her past for her choices she makes. So often I hear Christian women today saying something to the effect of, "I would do, go, be, but my past, but my husband." Scripture doesn't say her husband makes a lot of money; there is no mention of her looks or even about her past. She is valued because of who she is and for what she is doing in the present and for what she is doing to prepare for the future. I believe a godly woman is the glue that holds the family together.

Step 3: Enrich others by your life. Proverbs 31:11-12 says, "Her husband can trust her, and she will greatly enrich his life. She will not hinder him but help him all her life." Genesis 2:18 says, "And the LORD God said, 'It is not good for the man to be alone. I will make a companion who will help him.'" This word used for *help* is the same meaning as when Scripture talks about the Holy Spirit being our helper.

I believe behind every truly successful godly man is a godly woman. Belittling a man's abilities will only cause him to only fail, but when a godly woman truly believes in her husband God gave her, it gives her husband the courage to conquer the world. And together they will enrich others through their example.

Step 4: A godly woman needs to completely rely on God's strength to follow her godly desires. The Proverbs 31 woman achieved much through God's power. The following are my modern-day paraphrases of just some of the things the Proverbs 31 virtuous woman did. It states that she had employees; she also planned her day to avoid wasting time her precious time; I like to think she multitasked. She was competent in real estate and in the stock market; she prioritized her health; she liked shopping for bargains (my personal favorite!).

She didn't let herself get burned out, she was creative, she feared God, and she wasn't stressed out about the future of her family.

The Bible, in Proverbs 31, speaks of the "virtuous woman." Who is she? How does God in His Word describe her? Does she pray faithfully each day? Is she used in the gifts of the Holy Spirit? Does she consistently do daily Bible study and have regular devotional times?

The answer? I know you will be shocked, but none of these traits is listed in God's most extensive scriptural description of the Proverbs 31 "virtuous woman."

Now, please don't misunderstand me; there is no doubt that the excellent attributes listed above are valuable aspects of the lives of every Christian godly woman. However, God devotes almost an entire chapter of the Bible (Proverbs 31) to His description of the "virtuous woman." And the favorable traits that God lists are surprising to some readers.

I would encourage every godly woman to read weekly Proverbs 31:10-31 and ask God to show you through His word what He would have for you to learn. "Study to show thyself approved" (2 Timothy 2:15).

Happy Memories

I know that there were many things I shared that horrified you. Yes, my childhood was very hard and very traumatic. I do have some good memories, though, I promise. I would like to take the time to share what God showed me growing up. I saw God's handiwork in my life even through the pain I was experiencing. I have had several wonderful experiences in my life that I can see the Lord working in.

When I was nineteen, I worked in the same bus ministry that helped me as a little girl. I would go every Saturday to clean an elderly lady's house and ride the church bus with her every Sunday. Every week she would ask the church and me to pray that the niece who was taken away from her when she was five years old would be found. I would every Saturday look at albums of pictures of this baby that she wanted to find. I would listen about how much she loved and missed this girl. I told her I would pray for her.

I left for Hyles Anderson College and received a call from a friend back home telling me that my birth father was looking for me, so I went to visit him at my Christmas break. He told me as I was leaving his house I had to go visit my aunt's house; she was just dying to meet me.

I told him to give me her address and I would go see her right away with my friend. When I pulled up to the address given to me by my birth father, it was my elderly lady's house that I had cared for in the bus ministry. My friend told me maybe she moved; just knock on the door and find out.

So I knocked on the door, and the lady came to the door crying and saying she was happy to see me, but her niece was on her way. I asked her the name of her brother, and I began to laugh and cry because I realized I was the daughter of her brother. I was the young lady she was looking for all along, and I had been coming to her door for a full summer. God is so wonderful! I had been looking at baby pictures of myself and did not even know it. God works in wonderful ways. Most of the good memories I have are when I was in church serving in a ministry. I felt so much love from the church growing up.

Another good memory I cherish is my adopted mother, who taught me to read, would take me to the antique shops looking for a book series written in the early 1900 called *The Betty Gordon Series*; she would read each book to me at bedtime, and when we finished one, we would search until we found the next book. I loved and cherished these memories. I still have those books to this very day. I will never get rid of them, no matter how unreadable they become.

One time our garage flooded, and my books got ruined by the water; my husband could not understand why I would not just throw them out, for they had been ruined. I told him I have already heard the story but I was not holding on to them because of the book itself, but for the happy joyful memories they bring to me when I see them.

How Could I
Get Married after
Such Abuse?

Many have asked me how I can be happily married after such severe sexual abuse. Well, I have to say that it is not me; it is what I learned from God's Word that was taught to me from my stay at Hephzibah House. They taught me that if I did not want to grow up and marry what I was used to, which, in my case, was severe abuse, I needed to find someone in the church to help guide me to find my spouse who would be right for me and who would understand and not be abusive to me.

I took a lot of Hephzibah House's teachings and asked the Andrews family that I had come to love and trust to help me with this task in helping me find a godly husband. They agreed to help me with this. I told them I knew that I was not a virgin, but I wanted to find a man who understood and would respect that I did not want to have sex before marriage so that I could be pure with the man they helped me choose on my wedding night. I met my husband the first semester at Tabernacle Baptist Bible College. He had watched me from a window running in the pouring rain to class one night, and right before I got to the door, I tripped and fell into a huge mud puddle and had to run back to the dorm and shower and get back for class. He greeted me by holding the door open for me and asked me why I had a smile on my face, because he saw me fall right into that mud puddle. He said I looked like a drenched wet kitten. I laughed and said, "Why cry over spilled milk and over something I had no control over?" All I could do was get back up, run back to the dorm, and take another shower.

He would help me study before class many nights. I would rush in after working all day and try to grab a few minutes to study. I knew he would be there with his three-by-five cards studying. He had the best grades of all the students of the college. He came up to me after a chapel service one evening with a silk rose and asked if he could call me. I told him of course; that would be fine. Then after our first phone conversation, he asked if I wanted to go out on a date with him. I told him that he would have to call Mr. Andrews and talk with him and see if we could court. I explained to him that due to my past, I wanted to be courted, not just date someone. So Mr. Andrews told me to invite this mystery man over to Sunday dinner where Mr. Andrews took him outside and questioned and drilled him for over an hour about his beliefs, etc. And every time we saw each other, he gave me a silk rose. I used these dozens of silk roses to make my flower arrangements for my wedding.

The day I knew I was going to marry my husband was the day I tried to seduce him in the school stairway. I did everything I could to get my husband to kiss me.

He finally gently took my face into his soft warm hands and said, "Honey, I love you, and I want to kiss you, but I made a promise to you and before God that I would wait until our wedding night. I will not break that promise because I love you too much. Now when we say I dos, I am going to kiss you as much as you want."

I knew then that man was for me. I tested him; I would have kissed him too, but I knew that he loved me for me. It was not lust but true love he had for me. I knew he was completely trustworthy and an honorable man—exactly what I was looking for.

This wonderful family that allowed me to live in their home, the ones that helped me get my first job, taught me how to drive, helped me learn to trust again. Again, they took on a responsibility that they did not have to do. They truly were God sent for me.

I appreciate and love them so much to this day. I married my husband February 4, 1994. We have been married now going on seventeen years. I am so happy and so relieved to have a good, godly Christian husband who is understanding and loving to me at all times—someone who does not abuse me ever, someone who is my spiritual leader in the home, someone I can go to and talk to freely about anything my heart desires. I feel comfortable enough to tell my husband anything.

My husband and I are very close; I would have to say that we are best friends. The trust in our relationship is very strong. Does that mean we have a perfect marriage before God? I don't believe that anyone has a perfect marriage because we are selfish creatures by nature. We are human beings who make mistakes, but we are saved by the grace of God. Before I married my husband, I told him no matter how our lives turned out to be, divorce would never be an option for me. If we were to have problems, we were to choose to love and forgive and work through the problems, not seek out divorce. As you have read so far in this book, my husband had a lot to deal with when we first got married. He helped me struggle through many memories and triggers that hurt us both.

My husband was patient and learned and grew stronger in the Lord with me. I use and have chosen to abide by what I learned from Hephzibah House of what a godly wife is supposed to be. I don't argue or fight with my husband; I don't believe in going to bed angry at my husband.

I believe in complete open communication. Most important is if I am having fears or doubts, I talk with my husband; I never leave him wondering about what

I am feeling. He never criticizes or puts me down; he encourages me in the Lord always.

We have had four beautiful daughters; we have also had many children go to be with the Lord. We have eight children in heaven waiting for us to come be with them. I know right now my adopted mother is holding and loving on them.

I was still learning so much about this world when I married my husband. He has told me I have grown so much since we have gotten married. He has said many times that I reminded him of an innocent child when it came to knowing about this cruel world.

For example, my husband went into the gas station one time to get something for me to drink, and while he was in the store I saw this old man falling and stumbling and hurting himself, walking all crazy-like in the parking lot. I was pregnant and knew I could not help the man, so I got my husband inside the store and told him he needed to help this poor man outside. My husband came out and helped the man sit down in front of the store. He got into the car next to me and I asked him what he was going to do to help this poor man.

He said that the man was drunk and that was why he could not walk without falling down, and there was nothing he could do to help the man. He looked at me and asked me if that was my first drunk I ever saw on the street. I told him I never saw a drunken man like that. I had seen people get drunk at parties when I was a little girl, but they were all happy and such, not falling down and hurting themselves.

My husband explained to me that that man was the town drunk and stays so intoxicated that he needed rehab, that the man needed to want help before anyone could help him. So we prayed for the man before we left.

My husband and I have grown together as one. Our relationship has grown to be stronger in the Lord. I love him more each and every day. I praise the Lord for the family that helps find him. I praise the Lord that He has given me the opportunity to experience a happy marriage and a wonderful family of my own. I never dreamed that I could find such happiness.

We have had our challenges, our up and downs; don't get me wrong. Parenting in itself is a great challenge. Our children know that because of my past I don't like to discipline them because I never want them to grow up and say that I have hurt them in any way. So I leave most of the disciplining to my husband. But we are a team; we do discipline our daughters together according to what the Bible teaches us to do as parents.

I have to admit due to my past of severe abuse, I do and have struggled being affectionate to my daughters. I would give them hugs and kisses good-bye and good night, but other than that I had to remind myself it is okay to love and show them that I love them.

They know I am not a touchy-feely person, but they also know that I love them very much and that I would give my life for them. They mean the world to me.

Now many have asked me, "How do you have a normal sex life with your husband." Do I struggle having sex since I was so sexually abused growing up? I have to say in that area I did not have a problem because I had learned at Hephzibah House that the marriage bed is undefiled and that with my husband I was safe and it was right.

It also helps to have open communication with my husband.

Now, I think at first my husband was afraid to touch me because he did not want to do anything that would hurt me by bringing up bad memories for me. He was so loving and so understanding; we talked about it, and we just have grown so much in love that we have not had any problems in that area of our lives. What I mean by that is I never use sex as a punishment to my husband. I never withhold sex because I get angry at him. I don't believe in that. I don't believe God would be pleased with me to behave in such a manner.

I think the most important thing in a marriage is open communication with one another. Don't let sex be the core of your marriage. Let Jesus be the core! Sex is just a bonus.

I tell my husband everything. I keep no secrets from my husband, no matter how embarrassed I am or afraid of how it will sound. The one thing I can say about my husband is I truly trust and have no fears with him. I believe that is how it should be. I don't yell or scream at my husband; I don't believe in fighting with him. I don't believe in yelling because what is the point of yelling?

You say things you don't mean to when you're screaming and yelling at each other, and you can't take the hurtful words back after they are said to one another. I decided at the age of fifteen at Hephzibah House when I read in the Bible that "a soft answer turneth away wrath" (Proverbs 15:1) that was what I was going to do when people found it necessary to yell at me. So I have never fought with my husband, or anyone, for that matter.

I do believe what the Bible teaches, and that is that the man is the head of the household; the woman is to be submissive. I know to many *submissive* sounds like a horrible, abusive word. I believe that submission requires love, respect, and a willingness to *yield* to one another. Obedience, on the other hand, doesn't require any personal relationship between the one giving the command and the one obeying the command.

While a wife may obey her husband, if she does not submit to him, they will have a marriage more like an orderly military company rather than a loving and generous relationship with each other. A submissive wife not only brings order to her house, but she excels above a merely obedient wife by blessing her husband with the beauty of Christ—and everything pales in comparison to Christ.

Our submission is always a response to Christ. So we can do it with a smile, with gracious courtesy, and with godly determination. God makes the point very clearly that even though a person has done wrong in abusing us, we do not have the right to retaliate. Two wrongs do not make a right. God expects us to submit cheerfully as an act of faith.

I would encourage anyone who has grown up with any kind of abuse to be careful whom you marry. If you are afraid to get someone who will be like what you are familiar with in your past, get help finding that perfect someone to spend the rest of your life with. I am so thankful and grateful that I did.

Some people have asked me if my husband and I are going to help our daughters find their special mate. We are not going to arrange marriages for our children, but, Lord willing, when they get to the age to marry, they will be wise to listen to godly advice from their parents. We pray daily for them.

Steps I Take to Help Me Overcome Abuse!

There will come a time in your life when you have to decide that enough is enough. You must refuse to be held hostage any more by your mental, physical, or sexual torturers. You will want to move on once and for all. Fortunately, it is possible to overcome any abuse and regain your confidence and control that you may have lost to an abusive life. It will not be easy, but I assure you with God's help and guidance it can be done. These are the steps I had to take to help me overcome abuse.

Step 1: Dissociate Yourself from Your Past!

There is no point in lamenting about what has happened in your past. Cry your eyes out because your past is over. Then you have to wipe away the tears. No one cares about what you are feeling. I know that sounds very harsh and unloving, but it is true. When people look at you in this world, they are not going to understand that you were abused growing up. I am not saying that you do not deny your abuse either. Just accept that it has happened to you and that you are now on the road to recovery. You are a survivor! Now you must strive to become an overcomer. "Be not overcome of evil, but overcome evil with good" (Romans 12:21). What does it mean to be an overcomer? According to God's holy Word, an overcomer is someone who has suffered well. Overcomers are just ordinary people who have remained extraordinarily faithful to their calling, despite severe testing. It is very crucial to understand and keep fresh in our minds that overcomers are not defined by the outcome of their trial but by the process! An overcomer undergoes many painful situations knowing that they will endure their suffering through the love of Jesus Christ. A true overcomer remains faithful to God through all their trials. An overcomer copes with their problems, knowing they are not alone in their struggles. An overcomer will use their experiences to comfort and encourage others. You may not have exercised control over your past, but you can take charge over your own future from now on. Look at the past as lessons that point out what you no longer want for yourself. Be an overcomer!

It will take you time to heal from the abusive trauma caused by an abuser, but gradually you will learn and discover an inner strength and resilience to build a bright future for yourself that you never knew you had.

You will find as I have found that the times I thought I was the weakest were really when I was the strongest.

Remember God will never leave you or forsake you. A change in your environment may also be helpful for you to disassociate from your past. It is okay to leave and never look back. I had to do this with my adopted father.

Step 2: Cut Off Certain Relationships in Order to Heal

In order for you to heal, you must forgive your abuser, even when he or she has not asked for your forgiveness. This will help you with the anger you feel inside, and it allows you to heal and forgive yourself. This does not mean you have to keep that relationship alive. Sometimes the best thing to do is let him or her go and cut that person out of your life. I had to do this with my adopted father. My children will never meet him because I personally can't trust him. I forgave him for what he has done to me so I could heal. I will not allow my children to be abused by him or call him grandfather.

Step 3: You Will Need to Build Your Own Self-Esteem!

This will take time to do. I know this has taken me years to accomplish, and I have to admit I still work on this aspect each and every day. It will not just happen overnight. Your abusers are/were constantly hacking away at your self-esteem. I know my many abusers told me I could never do anything with my life. I was supposedly mentally retarded, remember.

When you come out of an abusive past, it is essential that you rebuild your sense of self-worth. You need to recognize that you can be strong in the Lord and that you are capable of independent thought. Remember that you can do anything in Christ. Be an overcomer, not just a survivor.

There is nothing that can or will hold you back from doing what you are meant to do in your life. Make sure that you surround yourself with people who value and support you spiritually.

This is an important part of your healing process. Form your own support group or join an online community that helps support its members to gain strength in the Lord. It is vital that you remember what makes you a unique and valuable lovable person. When you get married, make sure your partner knows about all of your past. I feel this is very important because you will have traumatic things happen that happened to you that will bring bad memories, and what a better support then your mate.

It is vital to remember that you hold the power over what you do in this life. Your abusers do whatever they can to gain power over you. Consequently, you will feel that you are being controlled and watched over every single movement that you make in life. You feel like people are judging you or putting you on the seat of judgment. You will fear making decisions for yourself, worried it will be the wrong decision to make. You will have to learn it is okay to make mistakes along the way. Just learn from them, dust yourself off, put your chin up, and try again.

You're only a failure when you give up completely. Through Christ you can do anything. You want to be something there is nothing holding you back.

I am thirty-seven years old, and I am still going to college because I want to be a biblical counselor. I don't care how long it takes me to accomplish this goal! With God's help and a very supportive family and husband, I will accomplish my dreams. I want to help people to overcome abuse in their lives.

The important thing is to understand that you are the only person who has power over yourself. One reason why you have been subjected to abuse is that you have handed your power over to your abuser. In most cases, you did not have a choice; you were beaten or made to do things you could not stop.

Some people find it hard to understand that fear can be the most powerful weapon known to mankind. A knife was not held to my neck nor was I chained to my home. Fear kept me in my abusive home even at the age of nineteen.

In reality, as an adult, no one can make you do anything if you do not let him or her. Realize that only you hold the power. Look for ways to empower yourself. I had to do this several times with my jobs as an adult.

My bosses would take advantage my inability to say no to them. I sometimes would turn to my husband for help and support but knew that he could not fight my battles for me. Only I could, with God's help, sit down and confront them and face my fear of conflict.

I had to learn the hard way that only you can know what is right for you! You are the only person who knows what is best for you. An abuser will want you to make decisions that are self-serving for his or her interest. However, such a decision may not be in line with yours or God's will for your life. As much as you care for a harmonious relationship, you need to take an alternate decision if your inner knowing tells you otherwise. Break the chains that bind you to their will. Find out what you want in life and go for it. Hence, it is your job to take care of your own needs. It is not about being selfish; it is about establishing certain boundaries for those around you. No one leads your life for you. Do what you know is right. Trust in God to help you follow through what is right for you.

It is very important to remember you can only control yourself. You can't control others around you. You can't change anyone but yourself. One reason that many women stay in abusive relationships is because they think they can help their partner change.

A period in time will lapse and they will find that they remain stuck in an abusive relationship and with no signs of improvement in their partner. The truth is that you cannot make anyone change; you can only control the way you react to them. I tell the teens that I counsel every day that you can't change your parents; you can only change yourself and your reactions to your parents. Instead, focus on improving your own life. In doing this you will discover your own self-worth.

You need to spend time setting boundaries and expectations for yourself. Sit down and write what your year, five-year, and ten-year goals are for your life. This is what I had to do when I got married; even before we got married I had discussions about this. People often expect a speedy recovery after being in an abusive relationship. If they do not allow themselves enough time to heal, they will often fall into another abusive relationship. It is clear to see that they have not learned their lessons.

They continue to attract the same kind of relationships that have them feeling needy. Hence, it is important that you spend time setting boundaries and expectations for treatment in future relationships before diving into a new one. Commit to a decision that you do not want to enter into any unhealthy relationship any more.

If you are clear in what you want, you are more likely to attract a loving and kind partner, unlike the one that you have been used to. Instead, find things to do that make you feel happy. Look at your life goals you set for yourself. Take a class or pick up a hobby. Try to recall what it is that you have always wanted to explore. With no one telling you what to do or holding you back, the possibilities are endless.

It is important to have a vision of who you would like to become once you have regained control of your life. If it helps, look for role models to follow. No longer will you be controlled without your permission. Most definitely, do what it takes to gain a sense of self-empowerment. And, most of all, remember there is nothing that you cannot do in the Lord.

Overcome Your Phobias/ Triggers from Abuse

Adult survivors of child abuse often struggle with many phobias. Many call it anxieties. I know I have and still do to this very day. Child abusers often silence their victims by terrifying them through a number of methods, including threatening the life of the abused child or someone he or she loves and cherish very much. Remember, fear is a powerful weapon. Until the adult survivor of child abuse chooses to heal from her or his traumatic past, repressed terror will continue to bubble out at unwanted times, often in the form of a phobia or trigger.

For example, children often have a phobia of certain smells because it will trigger a memory that harmed them in their past. Children who were confined as part of their abuse can grow into adults who have claustrophobia. The lack of control experienced as a child can manifest in a phobia of any situation in which the person is not in control. For me, it is confronting my bosses at work when they are mistreating me. Here is how to overcome a phobia after abuse.

Step One

Explore everything you feel when your phobia is being triggered. In addition to anxiety, what do you feel? Be as specific as possible. Don't hold back what you are feeling. I suggest getting a journal and writing your feelings down. Talk to God in this journal about your feelings you're experiencing.

You will feel like you are in some control of what you are feeling. If you don't want to journal, find a friend to talk to. For me it was my husband or a biblical counselor.

Step Two

If you have a reoccurring nightmare or dream, it is okay to take a look at your dreams. People with phobias often dream about the things that trigger their phobias. Record all of the details from your dreams into a dream journal if you need to. For people with post-traumatic stress disorder (PTSD), nightmares are often just flashbacks of their abuse. Some dreams may be hidden, pushed away memories. You can gain insight into the events that triggered the phobia through analyzing your dreams sometimes. For example, I had dreams of being burned alive. I had the same dream over and over for about a week until I sat down and discussed my fear with my husband. Then the dreams and the nightmares went away. For me, so did the bed wetting.

Step Three

Determine the source of the terror that you are feeling. This step might take some time for you, maybe for some even years. If you have been in therapy or counseling for a while, it is okay; this will not happen overnight. Phobias represent our deepest fears, so the source of the phobia might not reveal itself until you have been healing from your past for a while.

Until you determine the source of your terror, treatment is going to be aimed at the symptom rather than the cause. I had to learn that I had a deep fear of conflict. I don't like conflict. I did not confront the wrong done to me because I feared the conflict that it might bring.

Step Four

Accept that your reaction is rational. While your phobia might be an overreaction to an object or situation, the terror fueling the phobia has a rational basis. Once you connect the terror back to its source, your phobia will seem less odd to you, for example, my fear of dirt basements. I know where the phobia comes from; does this mean I have to go down a dirt basement and face my fears? I believe that if it was a matter of life and death and my child was hurt lying in a dirt basement, I could overcome this phobia.

Step Five

Take action to overcome the phobia if you possibly can. Doing something physical to overcome the phobia is empowering to you and may help reduce the fear of the trigger. For example, someone with a snake phobia might purchase a rubber or plastic toy snake and chop it into tiny little pieces. Save the chopped-up tiny pieces to view whenever your phobia has been triggered. My action to the fear of the dark is to leave on a night light.

I also keep a flashlight next to my bed so if the power goes out at night I don't have to feel afraid. I know my God is my protector. It is okay to make yourself feel safe. We cannot physically and emotionally heal if we cannot feel safe.

Step Six

Be patient with yourself. Overcoming a phobia takes time, for some, like myself, it may take several years and you will most likely never grow a fondness for the object or situation that triggers your terror. However, as you heal the underlying terror, the phobia will lose its power over you. It is okay to take steps to make yourself feel safe. Remember, God never gives us more than we can bear. God promises to never leave or forsake us.

Child Abuse Help: My Thoughts, Feelings, and Beliefs

If you are seeking child abuse help, it matters significantly what you think, feel, and believe. If you are an adult survivor of child abuse, you may still be struggling with these things. Contrary to what society or anyone else has told you, thinking, feeling, and believing are the essence of your being and vital to your mental health. I want to help you look into your troubling thoughts, feelings, and beliefs and discover what lies beneath them. Childhood sexual abuses and other forms of abuse have long-lasting ramifications and effects in one's life. You may be asking yourself, "Why me? How come God allowed this to happen to me? What did I do to deserve this?" Perhaps you are thinking, *I don't belong or fit in anywhere.*

As a child abuse victim, you may be experiencing feelings of anger, guilt, shame, unforgiveness, and loneliness, and you may not feel clean internally. These feelings are natural and are expected from someone who has suffered from abuse. You may feel that it's a burden to survive day to day. Put your trust in the Lord, and give your fears over to the Lord.

You may be even questioning your belief system: What do I believe? All this can be very confusing as you try to sort out beliefs about God, others, and yourself! So many who have been abused will turn to drugs, alcohol, and abusing others themselves because they do not know how to seek the help they need to heal from their own abuse.

Child abuse help is available to all who seek it. What happened to you as a child was totally evil and unnatural, but there is a supernatural way to deal with it, to be healed, and you can be transformed from the inside out. I know it is very hard; trying to cope with life, your thoughts, feelings, and beliefs is complicated, and I know from my own experiences it can be overwhelming at times.

There is no quick fix; I won't lie to you. There is no magic pill you can take that will take away the abuse. It will take you time, and it will not be easy for you. Your thoughts are still there, your feelings are still very much so present and believing and trusting people and yourself will be difficult at times. It's important, though, to remember God is there for you and He cares for you always. He wants to heal you and give you freedom from your fears.

Help is available for victims of child abuse. There is hope in Jesus Christ. This acronym was given to me at Hephzibah House. I found it when going through some old letters and a journal I had kept. I went from:

A: *Anger*: I am always angry at myself and mad at everybody.

B: *Belonging*: I am feeling very isolated. I feel that no one cares about me!

U: *Understood*: I feel like I am never understood. "Why me?"

S: *Shame*: I feel blame, shame, and guilt for everything that was done to me.

E: *Entrapped*: There is no way out for me. I am just surviving day by day, and no one can help me.

D: *Disgraced*: I feel that there is no love and no honor. I'm humiliated beyond possible repair.

With Christ's help I can become:

A: *Anger*: I now have righteous anger. I speak up for others as well as for myself. I don't sit back anymore and let people walk all over me.

B: *Belonging*: I belong to the family of God. I am very much so loved! I no longer feel like I don't belong.

U: *Understood*: I am totally accepted and cared for always by my heavenly Father. Christ love is shown to me each and every day.

S: *Shame*: My guilt and shame are all gone. I am forgiven in Jesus Christ. He took my shame on Himself. I no longer have to feel shame and guilt for my past.

E: *Ensnared*: I'm protected by God and His way. I can trust in *Him* always.

D: *Death*: Jesus died so I can be reborn in Him. There is no more disgrace, but God's grace instead! I am a sinner saved by the grace of God.

It is important to understand that the heart (our entire being) is a divine creation, and it is made up of our thoughts, feelings, and beliefs.

Proverbs 27:19 says, "As in water face answereth to face, so the heart of man to man." When a child is abused, whether sexually or otherwise, it goes right to the core of his or her being, the heart! The Bible tells us that out of the heart flow all things. Mark 7:20-23 says,

> And he said, that which cometh out of the man, that defileth the man. For from within, out of the heart of men, proceed evil thoughts, adulteries, fornications, murders, Thefts, covetousness, wickedness, deceit, lasciviousness, an evil eye,

blasphemy, pride, foolishness: All these evil things come from within, and defile the man.

Therefore, the heart is what is ultimately affected by abuse, and it needs to be healed. Only through God and His Spirit working in us can true healing be accomplished. Philippians 2:13 says, "For it is God which worketh in you both to will and to do of his good pleasure."

If you are dealing with child abuse that occurred in your past, you are not alone. Recovery from abuse is possible. I had heard about Jesus Christ all my life, but I never really knew Him personally until I went to Hephzibah House. I came to understand that sin separated me from God and that Jesus Christ was the answer to my dilemma. He became my Savior and Lord! He became my security and my protection.

Are you facing the regrets and hurts of childhood abuse? You are not destined to failure by the circumstances in your life—yesterday, today, or tomorrow. You are included in God's awesome plan of grace, mercy, forgiveness, and love. He is big enough to care about you with all your problems and your many scars. He is with you in every emotional battle you face on a daily basis. You are not alone with what you feel. He will guide you to a greater understanding of who He is and how He can save you. He is the way, the truth, and the life in every situation you are facing.

God cares about you, and He is intimately aware of what you are going through. He wants to help you forgive those who have used and abused you. One of the hardest things for me to do was to make a decision physically, mentally, and emotionally to forgive the people who caused me so much pain in my life.

Forgiveness played a key vital role in my healing process. I had to forgive myself first before I could forgive others. The abuse was not my fault, and I didn't cause it. Great healing then came when I forgave others.

Take away the I factor of your life and make it a God factor! Watch the changes that come!

My healing began with faith in God. When we pray to God for salvation, we're letting God know we believe that His Word is true. By the faith He has given us, we choose to believe in Him. Do you agree with everything you have read so far? If you do, don't wait a moment longer to start your new life in Jesus Christ. Who are you going to serve? Turn around what people meant for evil in your life and use it for the glory of God.

"But as for you, ye thought evil against me; [but] God meant it unto good, to bring to pass, as [it is] this day, to save much people alive" (Genesis 50:20).

They Meant It For Evil

By Grace Pennington

They meant it for evil, every scar and every tear.
They meant it for evil, year after year.
They meant it for evil, the torment and pain.
They meant it for evil, not for my personal gain.
They meant it for evil, the games that they played.
They meant it for evil, the price that had to be paid.
They meant it for evil, the abuse and neglect.
They meant it for evil, trying to take my self-respect.
They meant it for evil, each memory of them I bare.
They meant it for evil, never thinking these things
I would share.
They meant it for evil, the lies that they had told.
They meant it for evil, from the young to the old.
They meant it for evil, but I want to say,
Through God I was far too strong to give them
their way.

The goal I pray for you reading this book is to receive understanding on how to heal from your abuse. I pray that you have found Jesus as I have and have a personal relationship with Him. If you need someone to talk to or have questions you would like to ask me, you can e-mail me at theymeantitforevil@yahoo.com.

This is my beautiful family.

Faith   Lucinda and Stephen   Grace
Charity   Hope